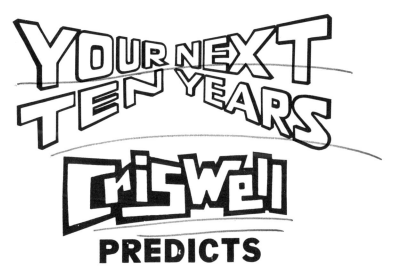

YOUR NEXT TEN YEARS

CRISWELL PREDICTS

by

Criswell

ILLUSTRATED BY
LEWIS N. SCHILLING, JR.

DROKE HOUSE, *Publishers*
ANDERSON, S. C.

Standard Book Number: 8375-6737-8

Standard Book Number: 8375-6737-8

Library of Congress Catalog Card Number: 72-79399

MANUFACTURED IN THE UNITED STATES OF AMERICA
BOOK DESIGN BY LEWIS N. SCHILLING, JR.

This is the second book by the man known simply as CRISWELL, a native of Indiana whose interests have carried him through many careers, from journalism to pre-med school. And always he has predicted events of the future with uncanny accuracy. (His first newspaper job was terminated when he wrote an obituary prior to the subject's death.) Until finally, predicting the future has become a way of life for him.

Criswell now lives in California, where he writes his famous "Criswell Predicts" syndicated columns. He is seen frequently on nationwide television programs. His introduction to this volume gives insight into both the man and his gift of prophecy.

The Future" covering the next thirty years until the date Criswell Predicts the world as we know it will end — August 18, 1999!

This book is more immediate. In these pages Criswell predicts the events that will befall America and the world during the decade of the 1970's. He also answers the 101-questions most often asked him about the next ten years. These predictions will affect us all, Criswell says — and if his record of 87% accuracy continues, then every person in the world has a personal stake in what Criswell predicts in this volume!

Dedicated To
My Wife
Halo Meadows

PREFACE

When I was a freckle-faced, red headed boy looking at life thru a picket fence in Indiana, I always thought I was something special!

In fact, the entire family, thought so too.

They classified me as a "freak"!

And perhaps a freak I have remained!

I had a vaulting imagination, and my searching wet noodle of a mind was hard to control.

I was not interested in the present events, but more interested in how they were going to turn out.

Everyone knew Mrs. Wentworth Hogginton was very ill, and would die, a fact that did not concern me. . .but which husband would she choose to be buried by for eternity?

Annette Jinsey ran away from her husband with a journeyman embalmer and returned two months later, three months pregnant. Who was the actual father, and could Annette be sure? Would Gus Jinsey be happy with Annette, and if she left the next time, who would she go with?

I became a prying busy body, horrifying the good citizens of Princeton, by merely asking questions "How do you think it will turn out?" and if I were not sharply dismissed for impertinence I would tell them how I thought it would all end.

Of course, when I was around no adult would even venture a statement about the weather, and I found myself isolated as what I said proved embarrassing to adult ears.

My peculiar point of view and my analytical mind which gave unmentionable facts without any slanted propaganda, made me a celebrity with several of the gossips of the town.

Grandma Wayne, who, after the birth of her last daughter at 35 took to a wheel chair and 50 years later was being wheeled by great grandchildren, knew more about the town than any one! She would say "Cris, walk by the Morritons and see if there is a blue Buick with a crushed right front fender parked there!" I would do this errand and she would exclaim "Frank Gurch is there again! Gus Morriton should know about Amy!"

7

The FBI or the CIA would have been proud of me, for I was an apt pupil! "How will this turn out?" Grandma Wayne would implore. I then would remark "Gus is going to come home early for lunch and shoot Frank and Amy!" This deduction proved true.

My parents were shocked at my opinions which I handed out like samples of soap, for I somehow knew of my gift of deduction. You start with facts, and then. . .

My Father, in a rather patronizing manner, told me it would be much better, at least for the present, if I kept my mouth shut and write my "Short History Of The Future" as I had so proudly called it.

I retired like a hermit to our attic, and wrote pages and pages about Princetonians and their futures, the results of their present activities. I saw nothing wrong in it, and blamed no one for any future action I had them commit!

I did not wish to be an unsung, unheard historian of the future, but insisted that I be permitted to read my short history of the future at the next family dinner.

The family thought it would be a dull evening, and the adults were passively polite.

I dearly loved an audience and I had them from the first.

With the talent of an attorney, I had built a case for all those mentioned, and with the finality of a judge I had passed a future sentence.

Each item was in three parts (1) background (2) the present and (3) the projected results.

I covered all of the personalities of Princeton. . .the kindly alcoholic doctor who performed abortions and the ladies he served. . .the widow of a former mayor who was known as "the traveling salesmen's delight". . .the Minister and the soprano and where they would meet secretly. . .how the butcher would thicken his pork sausage with cornmeal. . .how votes were bought beyond the brickyard pond. . . the never-talked-about drinking lady of the town. . .that artificial hand of an undertaker which he would thoughtlessly leave behind. . .the all night card game the high school athletic coach always ran. . .and the exploits of Miss Nellie who ran the beauty shop and loved to take baths with two men at a time. Names were given along with times and places plus my forecast of tragedies to come.

Had my "Short History of the Future" been published, I would still be serving time for personal libel and many good Hoosiers would have suddenly left Princeton for parts unknown.

The Family sat in a stony silence, too shocked for comment. The mind of a twelve year old boy can be a fearful thing! My Father took the manuscript from my hands and placed it gently on the open flame of the hearth. "Cris, wait until you are over 21 and away from home before you write another History of the Future!"

I am over 21, and away from home, and am writing another!

Cruswell

LET THE RECORD SHOW...

My predictions come true at an amazing rate. In my first book, *Criswell Predicts to the Year 2000!*, I predicted "the assassination of the nation's top Civil Rights leader" who, of course, was Dr. Martin Luther King.

And many other of my predictions in that book have come true or are coming true.

Many of the predictions in this book will refer the reader to my more expansive commentary on the subject in my earlier book.

Then, as now, I invite the reader to "keep record" of my predictions and see for himself whether these things come to pass.

Criswell

FOREWORD

O my Friend. . .

Let us pause for a moment!

For after us the deluge!

Our glittering world will soon be a smoldering cinder of a world!

The sins we do one by one are paid for two by two!

And in the next ten years, the story will be told!

Do not ask for whom the bells toll for it might be for you! Scientists tell us that we are a world of duplicates, triplicates, and trillionates. . .for this world and every item in it is duplicated a trillion times over in the vast universe of nearby space! Why should you feel lonely when you have a trillion counterparts? Do the other trillion feel as lonely as you? Are you fair to them?

The coming ten years may frighten you, but remember, of all the times to be alive, this is the time!

On this purgatory planet, I predict we will survive. But, while we live. . .the deluge!

Cruswell

CURTAIN GOING UP

Yes, my friend, the curtain is going up on the most exciting ten years of the 20th century! You have a front row seat. . .reserved just for you!
Of all the time to be alive, the time is now!
The orchestra is in an overture!
The actors, you and I, are moving into our stage positions!
The lights brighten. . .the music swells. . .and the curtain rises! You and I among every man, woman and child on earth are in the cast. . .all controlled by the Supreme Puppet Master Himself. . .and motivated by orders from above!
We are both the cast and the audience and the world is the theater!
We laugh at our mistakes and make our own jokes!
We are at the core of every crisis, every event and any joy!
We keep our eye on the program, and can hiss the villian and applaud the hero!
For that very villian and that hero is a part of you and me!
The marvels of the next ten years will seem like miracles to us now, but in 1980 we will take them all for granted!
On with the show!

CONCENTRATION CAMPS

I predict that the seven former World War II concentration camps (for detention) will be reactivated sooner than you may think! Over 50,000 people are in the country illegally and many of these are thought to be the fomenters of violence, rioting, murder and espionage! The President, through the Attorney General, with a simple signature, can re-establish these camps at once! And who will be the occupants? I predict they will be the proven enemies of the Unites States! Remember this prediction!

PLANTATION POLITICS

I predict it will be admitted, in open court, by many when they are questioned by "The True Negroes" that "Plantation Politics" (a method to enslave the Negro since 1865) was practiced to secure the vote, and keep the Whites in power! This charge will grow out of a civil rights disturbance, and be widely circulated for propaganda purposes! "The True Negroes" a splinter branch of the revolutionary Left, will grow in power, but will be spurned by many other minorities as a false representation! They will be frowned upon by the well known Negro Betterment Society as irresponsible radicals! Yes, in the decade to come you will hear much about plantation politics!

TINDERBOX

I predict that Mexico will become a tinderbox for America, as it will be politically controlled by Castro Communism within this period! Communism is communism in any form, just as it is impossible to be just a "little bit pregnant"! Yes, Mexico is a tinderbox!

STRANGER THAN FICTION

I predict that the coming ten years will be stranger than fiction! In the Grand Plan of the Lhama, in practical, yet mystic Tibet, the sign of the Tarot for the years from 1970 to 1980 is the Chariot! The Chariot is drawn by a black horse and a white horse, one is the negative force and the other the positive force of the Universe! There are no reins held by the driver, but these black/white forces are controlled by the mind, and the mind alone! We shall reach the mental peak of the 20th century in these years! The peak of science, invention, medicine, exploration and expression! We can offer no answer — all is clearly shown — no further bondage — triumph — personal liberty with the blood of heroes coursing through our bodies! Yes, I predict 1970-1980 will be stranger than fiction!

PANDEMONIUM

I predict that pandemonium will reign in Washington,D.C. with a wave of suicides of top government officials due to their proven treason, when they sold out the human race for red gold! We cannot break the law, we only break ourselves against it!

RED FLOWS THE RIVER NILE

I predict that red will flow the river Nile, due to the invasion of African nations in a sweep to the west! Not since Genghis Kahn have hoardes of fanatical tribes roared across Europe and the Mid-East! The Dark Continent will become the Red Continent — black with danger and red with blood! Let us stand by for the bloody battles!

CAMPAIGN FUNDS

I predict that in five years, all politicians running for office must list each donation and the amount in the daily newspapers so the voter will know who is backing him and why! Politics makes strange bedfellows and stranger givers of campaign money!

REBUILDING OF WOMEN

I predict a new science "Femology" (the rebuilding of women) will soon be most popular, where a woman can go into a free clinic and have her face lifted, a new hair line, reduce many, many pounds, have breasts reshaped and even a vaginal improvement! This new super-health-spa, with built-in diet and medical advice, will be a boon to all American women! Yes, there will be a national campaign of "rebuilding of women" in your life, very, very soon!

TRIUMPHANT TANGLE

I predict that a new wave of suicides among our youth will prove what a triumphant tangle they have made of their lives! They will know that they cannot fight the establishment. They are a part of it! The old fashioned precepts of God, Home, Mother and the American Flag are not old fashioned, but more alive, active and revered than ever before! The light in the forest is always there and we unconsciously walk in that direction! The night is dark and our youth is far from home, and it is our duty to at least point the way! The Establishment will never break, but people only break themselves against it!

NEW INSURANCE REQUIREMENT

I predict a new insurance requirement will be for all stores to have iron gratings across their front windows and doors for protection from looting, rioting and theft! These gratings must meet the new standard set by the fire and police departments. With the rising crime of theft your shopkeeper must make new moves!

THE NEW STUDENT RULE

I predict that new student rules of behavior will be set by college and university students themselves. And will be self-policing! The students of the law schools will be in complete charge! Any student in any protest of any kind, disrupting the flow of knowledge,will be tossed off the campus instantly. The new tone will be extreme conservatism!

BLACK HISTORY

I predict that Black History will be taught in all schools, colleges and universities, but will be included in the regular history course. When a separate study, even Negroes do not sign up for the semester! History is the dreadful record of our crimes, and Black History belongs in the many wrongs of mankind.

FUTURE ELECTIONS

I predict that all future national elections will be held at the same time by blending Eastern, Midwestern and Western time into one period, with all results fed by computer to the Big Board in Chicago, which is then instantly totaled and given to the nation at one time!

ASYLUMS WILL VANISH

I predict that asylums as we know them today will vanish in the next ten years! The advanced use of drugs, therapy and hypnosis will soon empty our mental hospitals and transform them into resorts for the Senior Citizens! Any American who becomes "disturbed" will be picked up at once, and taken to a free clinic where treatment is given at once! They will be detained for three hours and then released. No long or costly court procedures will be required! They are then placed on a "mental" probation lasting one month, and they must appear at the clinic on a weekly basis for that time! Yes, I predict asylums will soon vanish from our landscape and be replaced by very elegant retirement centers for our worthy senior citizens!

RESPECT WILL TRIUMPH

I predict respect will triumph and it will be a felony to transpose religious and national secular songs into other musical patterns, for either comic or insult purposes! The public will revolt against hearing "Eli, Eli," "Ava Maria," "Lead Kindly Light," "America" and "The Star Spangled Banner" sung in drunken psychodelic style, and will demand that Congress enact this new law for respect!

CRIME CONTROL

I predict that new theories of crime control will come thru automation! When some one is arrested, a full test of capabilities, talents and psychological and emotional conditions will be given them, and they will then be forced to carry out the directions of automation! The computers have a high degree of accuracy, and the individual is placed on parole! The directed course must be followed as to job, where you live, what you eat and your relaxation! The felon is automatically kept from further crime by the computer, which gives him a monthly examination! If the computer senses you need marriage, a suitable mate will be chosen for you, and you will be anchored to that person for life!

EXTRA INCOME FOR HOME OWNERS!

I predict that home owners and property owners will be able to have an extra income from attractive outdoor signs placed high above their houses or lots. These attractive, 3-dimensional signs, colorful and decorative will not offend zoning laws and will be permitted!

THANK YOUR POST OFFICE!

I predict that you will thank your post office for the improved delivery of mail in the very near future! Postal codes will be used to greater advantage and delivery will be speeded up! All mail will go by air at one set price! Your name must appear on your mail box and each place marked by numerals clearly! I predict the post office will also install "instant mail" where you can talk into an instrument, a typewritten letter to be received on the other end! Another service will be a photostatic copy transmitted internationally, for the price of a postage stamp!

HATCHING JACKETS!

I predict insulated hatching jackets for pregnant women! These new jackets, hermetically sealed to protect against extreme cold or heat, with built in medication and protection from pain, will be a boon to all expectant mothers! They will be smartly tailored in all the decorator's colors, to match the eyes and complexion! This will be a big seller in the spring and summer of 1975!

ELECTRICITY WITHOUT WIRES

I predict that electricity through wires will soon be a thing of the past! You will receive your electric power thru the broadcast system from a tiny box in your home! No wires will be needed! Your heating, cleaning, kitchen will all be by remote control. Your electric razor, vibrating machine, radio and tv set will all be wireless. A simple reading of the meter at master control will present you with the power you have used, and the cost to the penny.

All telephone calls will also be broadcast, from next door to the next country! Telephone poles will vanish and be an historical curiosity! I predict that someday your children will crowd around a museum case under glass and see the antiquated things we used in the 1960's!

FATAL MIXTURE OF TEEN AGE DRUGS

I predict that the present teen age drug problem will end in dire tragedy! The climate changes will make many drug mixtures fatal, and rather than becoming vegetables upon use, the person will be the victim of death! The drugs will effect the juices in the body, and a gurgling death will result! I predict that over one million teen agers will die from deadly drugs, which climate will make more deadly still!

WOMEN INTO MEN

I predict it will be a very common and inexpensive operation to change a woman into a man with the simple transplant of the sex organ! This grafting from a recently expired man, can take hold and not be rejected, as is a heart or kidney! A new series of male hormone shots can reduce the breasts, cause body hair to grow, the voice to deepen and the skin to roughen...and behold, a new man from the figure of a woman! The testis and penis can be grafted as easily as you would graft skin. Many women of an undecided mind can make the change!

SALARY FOR HOUSE WIVES

I predict that the Supreme Court will decide that any "house wife" is entitled to a weekly salary from her husband for taking care of the house, the children, if any, and other wifely duties! This will result in a complete rewriting of our divorce laws, separations and alimony! The entire tax structure for married couples will also be revamped! You can expect this change in 1978 or 1979!

INSTANT CREMATION

I predict that within five years you can be instantly cremated! Your body will be placed in a metal box, a tiny bomb exploded, and a thimble full of ashes will be all that will remain of your earthly temple! This can be placed in a shot gun shell, shot into the air, and you will be scattered to the four winds! The cost will be $100 complete, including five copies of your death certificate, a cremation permit and a memorial service! Your relatives or friends must deliver your body to the crematory. However, all movement of a dead body by public transportation will be denied, due to the heavy street traffic!

SECOND CIVIL WAR

I predict that within the 1970-1980 period, we shall experience a second civil war! The North will again march on the South! The South will grow in importance with a golden, never ending stream of oil, King Cotton and 1000% expansion of industry! The South will be the financial tail that will wag the Northern dog! The North will become so infuriated that arms will be taken up, and invasion planned and executed! Protest parades, meetings, sit-ins and student demonstrations signal the second civil war! Girls will be as anxious to serve as will boys! One militant group of Negroes will battle against another group of militant Negroes: one from the North and the other from the South! The Second Civil War will be financed privately by donations, as is a public election! Strange fish swim beneath the sea of the future waves of time!

GIRL SOLDIERS!

I predict another turn of events and custom in the 1970-1980 period. . .and that is female conscription. Many nations have tried this in the past, but the woman could always escape military service by quickly becoming pregnant! In the future that possibility will become extinct as the pill will be used, and women will have no escape or excuse! God pity the male soldier who must serve under a female general!

A SHOCKING MOON DISCOVERY

I predict you will be shocked when our American Astronauts find the ruins of a lost civilization in a remote section of the moon! A civilization far more advanced than ours. Your children and grandchildren will marvel at the age of discovery in outer space! We will have an actual visit to the Moon through our high powered television cameras.

SUPER DRUGS TO COME

I predict that among the super drugs to come into existance in the next ten years will be artificial coffee, tea, cocoa with a built-in nutrition and hang-over cure! "Brain food" for "brain fatigue" will be a best seller in 1975! Oxygen pills for depletion of energy will restock your system instantly!

NO DISCRIMINATION POSSIBLE!

I predict that a new iron-clad law, to be enacted by Congress and to be signed by our President, will make discrimination impossible! I predict that any job, any place, any where, can be held by either a man or a woman! Your fashion magazines will be filled with female impersonators and also male impersonators! Men and women will use the same rest rooms in restaurants, hotels, airports and think nothing of it! The next ten years will rid you of your shame, your shyness, your backwardness and also all modesty!

GERMAN SILENT AIRCRAFT

I predict that the greatest advancement in the next ten years will be the silent aircraft from Germany! This will make it possible to have air strips in any part of the land, without noise and vibration! These new jets will be so silent that even delicate listeners cannot pick them up. They will even evade the radar screens! Just as World War One and World War Two brought new advancement to aircraft, so will the next ten years! Aircraft will change overnight!

TIPPING WILL BE OUTLAWED!

I predict that within ten years tipping will be outlawed, and will be a thing of the past! This discriminatory practice of the master and slave complex has long plagued the 20th century and its time is now up! Panhandling on the streets will be a felony.

YOU CAN NOW DEEP FREEZE YOURSELF!

I predict that by 1979 you will be able to inexpensively and safely deep freeze yourself and be brought back to life in twenty years! The sleep will be deep, your organs placed in a dry ice dry-dock, and then slowly thawed out to your own dynamic rested personality! You can have this done at death or pre-death, as you choose, and the cost will be a nominal $5,000: the price of an average funeral! You will merely leave your possessions in the hands of the State, and while you blissfully sleep away, your investments will earn interest and profits!

HOW YOU WILL DRESS!

I predict that men and boys will wear a simple blouse and a skirt, which you will call "scotties". They will be comfortable and insulated for both heat and cold! You will wear furs, either in the stole or cape, with hats and gloves to match. Your shoe buckles will match your cuff links, tie clasps and ear rings! The color for men will be a scarlet red with a gold trim! Boots will be favored over shoes! I predict that women will wear paper thin tunics, which will cling lovingly to their figure as they walk! You will wear pastel colors only, leaving the bright hues to the men! Transparent cloth will be used to dramatize your figure, and all girls from 9 to 99 will scamper about in a new bright breezy fashion! The little girl look will be the thing! You men and women will dress more and more alike in tunics! The casual look, the youth urge, will overtake us all!

THE CANNIBAL COOKBOOK

I predict that the best seller of the 1970's will be *The Cannibal Cookbook*! With the rise of African culture, habits and living patterns, the consumption of human meat will be a common place thing — by other humans!

THE COMING DELUGE

I predict that the coming deluge will strike within the years of 1970 and 1980, hard, fierce and brutal! In the many predictions of *"The Next Ten Years"* I have indicated and pointed the way to many dangers and their solutions! A smile may be on your lips, but there can be terror in your heart! As Louis XIV said before the French Revolution "After us, the deluge!" but in our case it will be "While we live, the deluge!"

A MONO SUPER SERUM

I predict that a mono-super-serum will be evolved from the root of a well known American plant. As long as the Doctors and Scientists experiment with dogs and cats, they will fail in finding a solution! But when our miracle men of medicine and science delve back into the realm of American folklore cures, they will be successful, and only then! I predict a mono-super-serum which will make disease a historical curiosity within your lifetime.

OF ALL THE TIMES

Of all the times to be alive, I predict that the next ten years will be the most eventful and the most wonderful! We will have the 30 hour week. . .half of us will be taking some kind of course in free public education, with private schools and colleges fading into limbo. . .strict law and order thru a garrison law with a great freedom of movement and personal security for all. . .free public medicine for any ailment, most of which will vanish. . .a controlled price structure with all professions in hand with fixed fees. . .sound management which protects even the most minute area of our business world. . .undreamed of inventions which will stagger your imagination. . .the bypassing of war. . .but most of all, an abundant life. . .just for you! Yes, out of all the times to be alive, the next ten years (1970-1980) will be the most wonderfully eventful!

DANCING STARS

I predict that the world will soon see dancing stars due to the change of the winds which will give the illusion of this astral ballet! We will enter a new era in outer space on Jan. 10, 1970!

THE FIRST DIVORCE IN THE WHITE HOUSE

I predict that the first divorce in the White House will take place in the next decade!

31

EYES TURN TO JELLY

I predict that one of the top secrets of our Pentagon, whispered around Washington, D. C. will be a potent gas, which can be sprayed over a city, causing all of the inhabitants to have their eyes turn to jelly! This major breakthrough in destructive gas will be known within the next five years! All mankind is basically depraved!

SEVEN GRAINS

I predict that wheat, oats, barley, corn, buckwheat, rice and soy beans will be combined in one plant, easily raised, which will solve the nutritional problems of the world overnight! I predict that in the next ten years we will have combined farms under the strict supervision of the government! Remember the seven grains!

1970-1980
THE YEARS OF HEALTH & BEAUTY

THE AGE OF THE ANIMAL THERAPY — MINK OIL!

I predict that within the next ten years we will come into the age of the animal therapy, which our historians will record in bold, brazen strokes in the record of Science!

I predict that Medicine (Materia Medica) will become a pure science, due to the advances which will overtake us in a wave of progress. Swept aside will be the narrow minded concepts which have held us in bondage for so long.

I predict that the greatest discovery will be made from the lowly mink, the animal fats and oils and selected residue!

I predict that the center of research, development and marketing of Mink Oil products will be Orlando, Florida, where a new, dynamic company of young men will lead the way to a better future for us all.

I predict that the saturated mink oil will be the greatest cosmetic discovery since the Egyptians used olive oil! The fine, penetrating oil of mink, will act as a skin cleanser, a detergent to the soil left there by the very air we move in, and help to nourish and protect the skin!

The moment any one reaches the age of 17, their skin starts to deteriorate rapidly, and the oil of mink will help hold back the ravages of the advancing years!

I predict a soap made from the oil of mink which will instantly dissolve the grime of 20th century living, and leave the skin glowing with a renewed freshness which is difficult to believe, if not personally experienced.

I predict that this oil of mink soap will also be used in hospitals for pre-operation process, as it is so very thorough. It will come in a solid form, or as a paste or a lotion! For difficult deep burns and stains from gun shots, a powdered substance will be available! Deep scouring action can be used with this oil of

33

mink powder with amazing results!

I predict there will also be an oil of mink hair preparation, which will not only restore body to the hair, but bring back a youthful luster, and be an aid in restoring color!

I predict that many of the color shampoos today which sometime fail in their advertised promises, will have the built-in insurance of mink oil to make them fool proof.

I predict that the oil of mink will also promote the growth of hair, when rubbed into the scalp daily in tiny amounts, as it is so potent. A three weeks formula will be sold widely and the users will be a walking advertisement for all to see!

I predict the oil of mink will be the basis of all cold creams, skin foods and cleansing creams, hand lotions, bubblebaths, and spray skin protectors against the weather!

The oil of mink will also be used as the base of nail polish, which will nourish the nail and keep it from becoming brittle and cracking or peeling!

Last of all, but not least, I predict that the oil of mink will be used as a basic tonic for sluggish glands and will vitaminize and fertilize your system, awaking the sleeping glands which mean so much to your enjoyment fully of life! I predict that the oil of mink will be referred to as the "honeymoon" semi-restorative of vigorous living and sexual powers!

1511941

35

BY 1980

I predict through trend, precedent, pattern of habit, human behavior and the unalterable law of cycle that in the next ten years you will have travelled a full circle. . .and will have accepted the following incidents in stride:

THE SUPREME COURT OF 1980

I predict that by the end of ten years, you girls will take so much interest in politics, that you will hold many governor-ships, mayor-ships, senator-ships, police-captain-ships and industrial executive-ships, in fact the Ship of State! I predict that in 1980 we will not have nine old men on the Supreme Court – but nine old women! Remember this prediction!

OUR GREATEST PRESIDENT

I predict that History will record that our greatest Democratic President was Lyndon B. Johnson, who will tower head and shoulders above Wilson, Roosevelt, Truman, and Kennedy! LBJ really accomplished more social legislation than any other president to date! You will have been proud to live in the same momentous years as President Johnson!

HEARTBREAK IN BUCKINGHAM PALACE

I regret to predict that there is heartbreak ahead for Buckingham Palace! Many sleeping scandals will plague the Royal Family! The new anti-royalty movement of the Labor Party will bode ill! Ill health and death will soon place King Charles III on the British throne! Inner-quarrels will become public ones, and violent, disgraceful charges will be hurled from all directions! The Royal Family will not be any different than the quarreling family down the block from you!

BLOODSHED, BULLETS AND BATTLES!

I predict bloodshed, bullets and battles for Boston! Yes, that cradle of the American Revolution will again be another cradle for the New American Revolution! The Left will openly fight the Right! The Red Liberals vs. the Conservatives! You will see another Boston Tea Party where the Liberals will dump overboard the system which made America great! The Conservatives will defeat wave after wave of the Liberals in a long lasting era of bloodshed, bullets and battles. Within the next ten years this American Armageddon will happen!

MARRIAGE AND DIVORCE NEW STYLE

I predict there will soon be marriage and divorce by vending machine! These "courthouse vending machines" will be computer controlled, and a marriage license or divorce can only be issued if you are cleared at National Central! You and your mate to be will stand in front of the machine, deposit five dollars, a marriage ceremony of your choice will be played thru a recording, with appropriate background music, a handful of rice will be thrown at you, and you will be issued a small piece of cake and champagne! A divorce is granted the same way, but a stern moral lecture is given to you by a stern judge's recording. All facts concerning you and any one you want to marry will be stored in the National Central Information Bank and can be obtained instantly!

A MISSING SOUND

I predict that the jingle of coins (either plastic or metal) will be a thing of the past, for all money will be paper! This currency will be in the form of credit cards.

AMERICAN TRAGEDY 1980

I regret to predict an American tragedy on November 11, 1980! An instant newsflash from the White House will tell of the first suicide of an American president! This President will be popularly elected with much promise, but the Public will turn against him, and he will be the most hated official in all history. I predict that the suicide will take place in the lonely small hours of the morning. A shot will be heard, and upon investigating, his wife will find the sprawled body of her husband in his private office. A gentle rain will be falling, as will the tears of all Americans! The dead man did not fail us, we failed him!

YOU WILL BE FORCED TO MARRY!

I predict that you will be forced to marry to cement the economy of the United States! When people are married, they purchase homes, furniture, automobiles, travel more and live longer! Families of one or two children will be welcome, and larger families will be discouraged! Yes, I predict you will be forced to marry not only for your own good, but for the good of the national economy!

THE NEW BLACK AMERICA

I predict there will be a nation within a nation, a new Black America! Negroes will have their own land, banks, elected officials, schools, hospitals, universities, factories, stores, mortuaries, newspapers, magazines, laws on marriage, divorce, crime and punishment – all very separate from what is called the White Power Structure! They will also have their own Pulitzer Prize, TV-Radio programs and networks, Churches and Culture! No white heroes will appear in their history books, and only black statues will grace their boulevards. Separatism will carry the divine light of higher Sanction! (I refer you to my previous book *Criswell Predicts to the Year 2000!* for details of the setting-up of this state and its location).

THE DECADE OF PROMINENCE

This decade from 1970 to 1980 will see many men thrown into the light of prominence. . .Early in the period we shall have our attention called to a young harelip man from South Carolina who shall rise to prominence as a humanitarian. . .This young man will have made a great fortune for himself based on an idea, faith and enthusiasm. . .He will truly be a Sharecropper Ploughing The World. . .And he shall sow the seeds of great works for his fellow man.

ANOTHER BLACK PLAGUE

I predict that another Black Plague will hit the midwest with a shattering effect! I predict that there will be whispers that this epidemic is the forerunner of a planned germ warfare, and will terrify our population soon!

EPIDEMIC-OF-HEAD-LICE!

I predict that all America will soon face an epidemic of head lice! This will come from South of the Border! Due to climatic conditions, head lice have bred most rapidly, and this oversupply will find its way northward! Children and 'adults will be exposed to it!

A COMING AMERICAN TRAGEDY

I predict that a coming American tragedy will shock the world in about 20 years! I predict that the president who will hold office at that time will become incurably insane because of a brain tumor! This raving man will be restrained, and the White House will become a private mental institution. The Vice President will quietly assume all duties, and the business of federal government will continue as before! When Historians write of this event, they will marvel at the courage shown by the American citizens!

INNER EARTH!

I predict that future destruction lies within inner earth and not outer space, no matter how nearby space becomes! The undersea and underearth volcanoes will reap a harvest of destruction in 1972-1973-1975 never before witnessed by mankind.

A NEGRO TRIUMPH

I predict that the Negro will triumph under a plan to be issued by the Black Muslims where the industry, business, manufacturing, hospitals, drug companies and super-market chains will all be Negro owned and Negro operated! This plan, now in operation and off the drawing board into the action of today's tempo, will prove a triumph for the Negro!

HEADLINES OF THE FUTURE!

Business boom for the 1970's will be unsurpassed!...Stock Market looms as an international barometer for peace!...England, France, Italy, Mexico and Hawaii face race-rioting on bloody scale!...Red China executes dissenting students!...Supreme Court welcomes first woman judge!...War spending continues thru 1980!...Price controls stop damages of inflation!...New immigration laws very strict!...New Japanese automobile revolutionizes American market!...Bitter battle backstage in Negro leadership!...New gum infection results in rotting teeth epidemic!...New federal rulings on all savings accounts!...Russia enters new arms race with America!...Income property and land best investment!

NEW TAXES ON HORIZON

I predict a federal rent tax of 5% on all hotel, motel, apartment, dwelling and trailer courts by 1975! Too many people do not pay income taxes, and this will cure the fault!

BLOODY TIMES AHEAD

I predict that the Iron Curtain countries around Russia will face bloody times ahead, for Russia cannot permit anarchy! Blood will flow in the streets as never before by late 1972! Mass executions will take place publically as a warning to citizens to shape up to Communism or ship out to oblivion!

CAMPUS VIOLENCE

I predict that in 1971 the American public will be shocked by a series of flag burnings by students! This will not only take place in colleges and universities but also in local high schools! I predict that students will also call attention to their demonstrations with the hurling of pet dogs and cats into bonfires to "spite" the American way of life! Yes, 1971 will be filled with thoughtless actions by thoughtless young Americans! However, I predict stern local action to combat these actions will take place, spearheaded by the American Legion!

CONVICT DOCTORS FOR LIVE TRANSPLANT

I predict it will be proven in court in 1971 that the heart of a living human being was lifted out for a transplant! The Doctors will be charged with first degree murder! This shocking court case will blaze across your front pages!

PREDICTIONS FOR 1973

I predict that raw tobacco leaves will be found to have a new medicinal value. . .that France will demand that all underwear for both men and women be made from nylon, not cotton or silk, in a new national plan for manufacturers. . .that a grape brandy will be sold in pellet form. . .that England will refuse entry to all citizens of other countries unless they deposit one year's expenses for food, clothing and taxes. . .that West Germany will be the new tourist haven due to the new bargain in marks. . .and that motion picture distributors will refuse to distribute any film degrading any white person! This has been true in Europe, and will now reach our shores!

YOU ARE WHAT YOU BREATHE

I predict that at one time you were what you ate, but now you are what you breathe! The vitaminized foods have taken care of your diet, but now the danger to your health comes from the air itself! Dirty, deadly, poisonous air is now reaching your lungs — every moment — awake or asleep! I predict that after a national Black Friday in 1973 — when many, many will die from suffocation — something will be done very quickly!

MAGNIFICENT MIAMI!

I predict that magnificent Miami will become more magnificent than ever, with the present secret plans of the Chamber of Commerce! The "tourist traps" will be eliminated, and a fair pricing act will be placed into effect, which will make Miami the number one vacation spot of America, far outreaching California, Hawaii, and other present attractions!

CRISIS IN ASIA

I predict that within ten years you will witness the great crisis in Asia when Red Russia joins Red China to give the world a red blood bath!

THE TAX ON ENGLISH PROSTITUTES

I predict that england will be so hard pressed for new ways for taxes, they will demand a sales tax on each love transaction by prostitutes, to be paid at the end of the day! A list of customers must also be filed!

CONTROLLED INCIDENTS

Just as Napoleon created circumstances, we are moving into a world of controlled incidents! I predict that within the next ten year period we will have "controlled weather," "controlled economy," "controlled professional charges" (doctors, lawyers, dentists and engineers) and a controlled political world!

A NEW DEATH RAY

I predict the completion of a new death ray which will kill unborn children by rendering every man and woman sterile.

INTERNATIONAL

I predict that the ghost of Napoleon will again be seen near his tomb in Paris, which superstition has, will bring on another French disaster! On the eve of the Maginot line invasion by the Germans, the ghost of Napoleon stalked the area! Another national tragedy for France!

POWDERED PINEAPPLE

I predict that your next savory seasoning will be powdered pineapple, to be used in all cooking, from meats, dressings, puddings, salads and even to sweeten coffee or tea!

THE STRANGLING, CHOKING DEATH

I predict that on a quiet Sunday afternoon, the sulphuric gases from outerspace will sweep the world when it passes through a gas belt. This gas will strangle and choke to death millions of people. Animals will survive for they will bury their noses in the dirt, but Man will perish in great numbers, for he has been softened by 20th century civilized living! Once man faced this same element, but survived, but this time Man will perish! Date: June 25, 1978.

A NEW RACE

I predict that the new race of man, which will appear after August 18, 1999 – the end of the world – will crawl on all fours, with our hands and feet becoming claws for physical protection!

AMERICAN HAVOC

I predict that there will be American political havoc in 1976, when there will be *four* well established political parties rather than the two we now have! There were four parties in 1776! Just 200 years ago!

A STRANGE PREDICTION

The Indian Tribes of Nevada, through their Medicine Men predicted: "The burning sun will blanche the bones of many natives, and the searing heat will result in death and in destruction in valley after valley. Huge underground lakes will appear and make the desert bloom!" This legend of the Nevada Tribes proves to be a carbon copy of the geologist's report of long standing! The time: 1979!

RIOT TORN TEXAS

I predict that riot torn Texas will declare garrison law – within three years! The new drive for revolutionary students into the colleges and universities will bring the proud state of Texas this point!

ERIE PENNSYLVANIA

I predict that Erie, Pennsylvania will be come the boom town in the Northwest portion of the state! A new Civic Center, huge apartment houses, new resorts along the Lakefrontage, but most of all new industry, will boom the area in the 1970's!

HEADLINES OF THE FUTURE

Storms batter Atlantic Coast!...Bitter backstage battle over rent parity!...Death on the Supreme Court shocks the nation!...White House becomes fortress!...New automation locates missing people!...Price fixing on all imports!...Vending machines offer new postal services!

CHILDREN OF THE MOON

I predict that the French countryside will be terrified by what they call "children of the moon" — scamper at the sight of a human, but are visable both during the day and the night. Scientists agree that these sightings could very well be from outerspace.

SECRET GRAVEYARD

I predict that a secret graveyard will be discovered near Denver, where murdered men and women were buried unquestioned and for a fee! Many riddles of Denver will be solved when the identity of those buried are known. New scandals will arise!

THE LAST BATTLE

I predict that the last battle is slowly shaping up in the Middle East. We marvel from day to day how Biblical Prophecy is slowly working out! You will soon see the last battle, for even the Geologists tell us we are in the time of the end! The space between is but an hour, the frail duration of a flower!

HIGHWAY SLAUGHTER

I predict that highway slaughter will increase by 100% in the coming ten years!

HUSH HUSH SCANDAL: 1970

I regret to predict that one of the most famous Hollywood figures will soon be behind the bars, due to his falmboyant love affair with his own daughter!

THE DECADE OF GOOD WORKS
THROUGH COMMUNICATION

I predict that this decade shall bring forth many good works by a dedicated few people who shall bring to us a message that is explicit: God lives through man's Good Works. At the very center of this network for the communication of good works will be the national chain of motels!

MAN AND REASON

Man will let the computer reason for him, and free man for the creative role which the computer can never master.

THE WRITING AND PUBLISHING OF FICTION

There will be a totally new concept of publishing arrangements between authors and publishers. It is now being born in the mind of two young, unknown publishers and will allow them to compete with the giants of the industry. It will double the number of books on the market and will bring about the greatest change in 100 years in the field of publishing.

HOMOSEXUAL CITIES

This prediction is covered fully in my first book. It is already beginning. It shall become reality in the 1970's.

HALLS OF CONGRESS

I predict that the Halls of Congress will soon reek with a stench of an international sell-out by some Senators and Congressmen. This monstrous crime against the American people will not go unpunished, and many political careers will be wrecked!

TERROR BY NIGHT

I predict that Mother Earth will suffer terror by night thru a cosmic display of shooting stars and meteors which will light our midnight skies for a full 24 hours worldwide! I predict that on August 27th, 1973, the scheduled fireworks of the Heavens will take place, and even our most Atheistic nations will fall to their knees in deadly fear of these natural events! An astral explosion in outer space, scheduled for over 1,000 years, will be upon us! Remember the date: August 27th, 1973!

THE ARROW AT NOONDAY

I predict that assassins' bullets will strike their mark like the arrow at noonday, and bring to earth many leaders all over the world! The Destructionists who prefer Anarchy will plot and plan this very thing to happen in front of your very eyes! Just like the Kennedy killings were on camera, these new killings will be witnessed on your tv screen!

RUNAWAY CHILDREN

I predict that 1970-1980 will see more runaway children than any years to date! This is the first television generation! Boys and girls will take to the road in great numbers, and they will be gathered up by a police net and returned home, only to leave again! They will be found in ill health, narcotic addicted, diseased and mentally damaged.

A FRIGHTENING DISEASE

I predict a new loathsome plague out of India, one so mysterious and frightening that it will stagger the imagination of 20th century citizens. This deadly disease is of the rampant leprosy family, is rapid and actually devours the human body piece by piece! This highly acid ailment eats away at the flesh and bone, leaving nothing in its wake!

CRISWELL PREDICTS
NEWS LETTER FOR 1979

Here is your newsletter of the future dated 1979: Land has become so valuable that the single occupancy dwelling has almost vanished. Tall apartment buildings with individual balconies have replaced even the smallest hotels and rooming houses! The greatest change is the department stores, reaching into the sky, with moving sidewalks which take you to all floors — you may select the item you desire, it will be wrapped and waiting for you at the exit! There will be a beauty salon where you may have your face instantly lifted, and your hips reduced by ten pounds in ten seconds, your teeth cleaned and cavities filled, and a sonic shampoo! A Dress Emporium where a dress is automatically designed for you, fitted to your figure all in ten minutes! And if it does not do the best for you it is rejected by automation instantly! Your husband can regain his high school boyish figure in a special men's department and receive his beautification also with a hair transplant! The area surrounding your department store of the future will all be high rise apartment hotels-motels, all own-your-own amid parks and pavillions! The store will carry everything from cradles to coffins! Everything that you will need in your entire lifetime! In fact you could be born here and never leave! Your department store of the future will be a city within a city within a city!

A VERY FAMOUS PREDICTION

When Nostradamus in 1548 published his *Centuries*, he brought the wrath of the Gods on his own head for he predicted: "In time to come, huge birds, man made, will fly over London and drop flames which would destroy the city!" This seemingly far fetched prophecy scared people then, and they all started moving to the outskirts! (This came true in 1944-5 on the buzz bombing by the Germans). He also predicted "The Royal Family of England will hold power from Elizabeth to Elizabeth!" (The Empire did hold world power from Elizabeth I to Elizabeth II and then seemingly fell apart!) "Machines will do man's thinking, his scheming and his planning!" (We are far too much controlled by automation! And we are fast becoming slaves to the machine age!) "In the future it will be possible to run away but you cannot hide!" (With our social security number, our fingerprints on file, and the rapid instant flashing of news, we cannot vanish if we all wanted to!) "The span of man will be doubled and crowded conditions will exist all over the world". (Man only lived to be the average of 35 in the 15th century but now the expectant age is near seventy! There is great danger of a new population explosion, which could not possibly have been imagined then!) But perhaps the most famous of all Nostradamus predictions were in verses where he actually mentioned the names of Hitler, Mussolini, Franco, the Duke of Kent, King George V and the Kaiser — and foretold their fates centuries before they were born! A fantastic man, this Nostradamus!

ANOTHER FAMOUS PREDICTION

A Mayan Tribe, long since departed from Earth, has left a strange prophecy, and we quote "It will be found that the individual can change sexes by a potent drug and a simplé routing of the flesh! Women will become the Dominant sex, while the men will become womanish, even to the gift to bear children!" Even H. G. Welles in his *Things To Come* hinted at the day when Men would be Mothers! The interchange of sex was nothing new to the Romans and Greeks, and even today we have adherents to this once most common practice! Yes, The Mayans predict that men will become mothers in our century!

A VERY TOP SECRET

I predict that this very top secret will soon be made public: The use of doubles where famous personalities are concerned! It is a whispered fact that the Royal Family, DeGaulle, Kozygin, Franco and Castro all have used identical doubles to be photographed from afar or appear in parades with the public none the less wiser! I predict that we in America, due to the many attempts at assassination, will revert to the European practice of employing doubles for our heads of state!

THE BITTER TEA OF MAO

I predict that misfortune favors no man, and Mao, the present patron saint of communism out of China, will find that his health, that most precious possession of humanity, will decline, and at the peak of his power, be forced to drink bitter tea! A lifetime of effort, at last success, then the terrible truth of an incurable illness! This atheist will return to the God of his fathers!

HOLLYWOOD!

I predict that Hollywood Boulevard will become a Mall where the great and the near great will mingle! Waxen statues of your favorite star in glass capsules will greet you every ten feet! An afternoon and evening movie will be shown on large screens placed every block! Food and Cocktails will be served in the open, and Hollywood will come back into its own!

TERROR AT NIGHTFALL

I predict terror at nightfall for the Hudson Bay Area of Canada! A sleeping volcano will errupt causing havoc, death and destruction to the majority of inhabitants of that sad territory! The earth will buckle with geysers of fire shooting high into the sky which can be seen as the Northern Lights as far south as Texas or Florida! This will be only one of the major natural disasters in this ten years!

A FABULOUS NATION REVIVES

I predict that a once fabulous nation will revive, Armenia! This tragic nation will have a new lease on life and will again return to former glory! A new wave of nationalism will place Armenia in world banking circles once more! 1976!

DELIGHTFUL. . .DELICIOUS. . .HUMAN FLESH!

The following prediction, based on trend, precedent, pattern of habit, human behavior and the unalterable law of cycle. . .has best not be read by those who have weak stomachs! A friendly warning to prevent nightmares and traumas!

If any one in your family is easily influenced or susceptible to fright and horror, it is better that you hide this volume from them.

In 1975 and 1976, mortuary burial practices will take a strange turn − that of freezing the dead body for later revival.* This will never be completely a success, and although there is only minor brain damage, organs of the body will not function normally when partially revived.

Mentally, the revived individual could not comprehend the events taking place. Some are sad, pitiful creatures to behold!

A strange and loathsome cult will come out of Patoka, Indiana. Some will say they are decendents of the Patoka Tribe of Indians, while others claim they were the Devil's Own! These crazed men and women, and some children, will raid the Morgues where these bodies were kept at frigid temperature, steal the bodies, and devour them. They are brittle and can be eaten like crisp ice cream cakes. Delightful, delicious, human flesh! This cult will soon spread from coast-to-coast, and thousands upon thousands of frozen human bodies will be eaten with relish. This cult will be known as the "The Frigids". Even the bones will be eaten. And the rare delicacy will be the skull of any one under 18!

---

*Cryogenics, the art of freezing a dead body for later revival. Many famous men and women who died in 1969 have secretly had this done. A costly procedure and still unproven.

Lungs, livers and genitals will be particular favorites.

So ravenous are the Frigids that morgues will be guarded by the National Militia around the clock, to protect the sacred frozen bodies of the dead.

It will not be uncommon to see someone walking down the street daintily crunching a mouthful of a frozen person.

The Law Enforcement Agencies will stand by and permit this dreadful activity due to "freedom of desire" and the new and vicious attitudes of the Liberals.

The Supreme Court will hand down the decision that "no harm could come from eating dead frozen flesh of humans" and that the "Frigids are in their constitutional right as the dead body could not object and was passive, feeling no pain!"

This fad of frozen flesh eating will continue on until August 18th, 1999, in spite of squeamish individuals who would rather see it stop.

In fact, it will stop on that day with everything else, for I predict the end of the world on August 18, 1999!

TEN MILLION POISONED PEOPLE!

I predict that tragedy will again strike the Ukrainians! Once, starved systematically by the Red Masters of the Kremlin, Mother Nature will poison ten million people thru a deadly gas escaping from the bowels of the earth into the vegetation! There will be no living to bury the dead, and the entire population will die within three horrible days and three horrible nights! An atomic bomb will be the funeral service and the disposition of the corpses as there will be no other way! This shocking event will happen in July 1977!

THE GREAT TIDAL WAVE

I predict that the great tidal wave will hit regions of Asia destroying parts of Yemen, Saudi-Arabia, Iraq, Iran, Pakistan, India, Burma, Siam, Sumatra, China, Borneo and half of Australia! The great tidal wave will be caused by a huge meteor which will crash into the very center of the Indian Ocean. Millions will perish on April 10th, 1975.

20TH CENTURY NAPOLEON

Just as the predicted 20th Century Charlemagne in the person of Charles DeGaulle brought France back from the inglorious level to which she had sunk, I predict that a 20th Century Napoleon will revive the French National Spirit after the Bastille Day of July 14th, 1979! This man, like his counterpart, will be an Italian and be a decendant of Christopher Columbus from Genoa! This young man, now living in the beauty of the seven hills of Genoa near the Composanto, born in 1959, is awaiting his cue to enter on the stage of history. He is waiting in the wings, a very poised but thoughtful young man!

THE RISE OF ATLANTIS

I predict that the sunken continent of Atlantis will arise from the briny depths of the Atlantic Ocean on May 6, 1987!

THE RISE OF PACIFICA

I predict that the sunken continent of Pacifica will arise from the briny depths of the Pacific Ocean exactly one year later on May 6th, 1988! Forbidden secrets of a long dead civilization will be there for all of us to know on May 6th-1987-88!

A MONARCH WILL VANISH

I predict that a Monarch will vanish in Iran and they will find him cruelly murdered which will start a Mid-East war! A finger of guilt will be pointed, but nothing proven!

THE GOLDEN SANDS

I predict that the next gold strike in the world will be in Saudi Arabia, where pure gold will be found generously sprinkled in the golden sands! This will be the biggest gold strike on record and will stagger the imagination of all mankind!

A NEW SHRINE

I predict a new shrine will be discovered with miraculous healing powers in Ankara Turkey. This new shrine will be surrounded by a powerful light, unexplained.

MONGOLIAN REPUBLIC

I predict that the Mongolian Republic will turn the clock back 2,000 years and revert to the feudal system.

THE HOLLOW CROWN

I predict that Spain will again become a monarchy but the King will wear a hollow crown! The outdated pomp and ceremony, costly tho it may be, will remain a part of the plan of bread-and-circuses for the public! I predict that the Bourbon princelingwill remain a figure head but a symbol of all that is past! His death will come on swift wings thru a boating accident in 1975. The power of Franco will survive!

WAKE UP YOUR SLEEPING HAIR!

I predict that you can wake up your sleeping hair with a partial transplant, in small squares, which evens up the hairline and completely covers the bald pate! No one is hopelessly bald and beyond help thru this new method! The use of mink oil applied cosmetically to the sleeping scalp can do wonders although hair differs greatly in individuals!

A SUICIDE CLUB

I predict that a famous European Suicide Club will seek members among the students here in America! Numbers are placed in a hat, and the one drawn must destroy himself by fire in protest to some encroachment on a fancied political wrong to the New Left! American students have not responded as the Kremlin based Society had expected!

THE SHATTERED STAR

I predict that we will soon have heavenly fireworks due to a shattered star, which will cover the entire sky with tiny smoking, trailing comets! Somehow this will convince many people that "God is not dead" but merely a little displeased at the antics of His children here on the planet Earth!

THE SOLUTION TO CAMPUS RIOTS

I predict that the solution to campus riots will be found thru the "swearing in of all students and teachers as deputies" and then if there is any rioting, this immediately becomes a first degree felony, with instant arrest and a non-attainable bond! This was the solution to many foreign university riots, and it is guaranteed to work in America!

THE REVOLT OF THE TAX PAYER!

I predict that tax payers will revolt until they have the adequate police protection against robbery, mugging, murder and personal danger in 25 of our cities from coast-to-coast!

CITADEL OF SILENCE

I predict that Congress and the White House will become a citadel of silence, and then they will release a joint-plan of action! Just as President Roosevelt took stern action in 1933 for our national and international ills, I predict we will all rally around our present presidents. Look for an active ten years.

THE MIND MACHINE

I predict that the treatment of disease will be carried on thru the mind and the mind alone. When you become ill, an electric cap is placed upon your head, and vibratory power is sent to the ailing portion of your brain!

I predict you will be wired up like an artificial kidney, and you will survive!

The mind is the basis of all conditioning of the body. . .and it is to be proven medically, that you are what you think!

I predict huge medical-mind centers will be sold on a franchise basis, as this simple machine can accomplish miracles where medical science has so far failed!

I predict these medical-mind centers will be as numerous as hamburger or fried chicken restaurants, and they will dot the countryside of America!

A VERY FAMOUS PREDICTION

Almost 500 years ago Agatha Shipton lived in Creswell, England and was given to rhymed predictions such as: "Around the world thoughts shall fly, In the twinkling of an eye" (radio, tv, telephone) "In the air men shall be seen, Floating in space, where none had been!" (not only does this include aircraft, but our present space explorations) "Carriages without horses shall go, and accidents fill the world with woe!" (the automobile and the rising carnage on our hiways) And 200 years before the Revolutionary War she stated, "Far over a wild and stormy sea, A race shall gain their liberty!" and for the 20th century she merely states "Taxes for blood and war, Shall come to every door!" Yes, Mother Shipton is proving to be correct again, tho we hate to admit it!

SERVICE BY MACHINES

I predict that your children will receive service by machines! Their homes will be cleaned and dusted. . .their lawns kept in neat order. . .their clothes fresh. . .and their lives regulated even as to diet, dental work and repair! Altho they will have no idle moments, they will be assigned by the State to do certain duties, which they cannot shirk or death results! The plug on their machines will simply be pulled — oblivion!

RELIGIOUS REVIVAL

I predict that by next year an amazing religious revival will be in full swing. "The Old Time Religion" of twenty five years ago will come back into fashion! The key of this will be faith healing, revival meetings and song fests! Yes, all America will again hit the sawdust trail next year!

REBUILD THE BODY

I predict that you will be able to rebuild your body by a strict set of mild exercises, a carefully planned diet, a little more rest and a more positive mental attitude! This new plan set forth by Doctors for those over 35 will work amazing miracles! Yes, you can and will rebuild your body! Personal health will be the number one concern!

YOUR TRIP TO EUROPE!

I predict that within five years you will be able to take a trip to Europe by air for only $100 Round Trip from New York or Los Angeles! You may also book your tour, your hotel and meals at the same time with the same ticket!

MANY PEOPLE ASK:
"ARE YOU FEARFUL OF THE FUTURE?"

Many people ask me "Are you fearful of the future, for you know what is going to happen?"

Frankly, I am not! The future is merely the continuation of the past abridged by the present.

It will never be any later than it is at this moment, and another second has ticked away bringing us all nearer to Eternity!

I predict that we will all grow in Faith, religious memberships will boom and a renaissance will take place in the next ten years.

Those who seek to destroy sentiment, seek to destroy all America. There is nothing outdated about God, Home and Mother! Christmas, Thanksgiving, July Fourth, Labor Day, Valentine's Day and Armistice Day are sentimental peaks of the year!

There is a God.

There are no Athiests at the funeral of a loved one!

Yes, there is a God, and One with God is always a majority!

And it is God's will that prevails — even to the end of the world as we know it in 1999!

LIVING RIGOR MORTIS

I predict that it will be entirely possible for you to have rigor mortis while still living!

Rigor mortis is the stiffening of the muscles after death, from coagulation of the protein, starting two hours after expiration and lasting up to six days.

The chemical balance of the body will be tilted by our impure air and can result in rigor mortis while you still live.

Unless quick action is taken, it will be fatal.

Just another fearful result of man's impure environment which he has defiled.

UNSPENT TIME

I predict that it is entirely possible for you to bequeath and will to someone your unspent time at your death!

A new insurance policy soon to be issued, will permit funds to be paid to someone you wish to honor after your death, with full expenses on some trip which you could not take!

This insurance policy will be listed in your estate as top priority, and cannot be cancelled by the whims of your relatives or the executor!

It will be pre-paid out of your estate. . .a most wonderful gift. . .of your unspent time. . .plus expenses. . .for a very dear friend! You can bequeath your unspent time!

GLAMOUR IN THE FORMALDEHYDE SET

I predict a new glamour in the formaldehyde set with the Royal Funerals for $1,000! The corpse is dressed first in a slumber robe for the first viewing. For the second the corpse is dressed in every day fashion, as you saw them in life. For the funeral on the final day, the corpse is in formal attire as though attending a social function. Both men and women will wear hats which give the appearance of leaving on a journey. The next stop will be the Golden Shores! You will always remember the dignity and the honor paid the corpse in the coming Royal Funerals for $1,000! A sacred cremation may also be secured for those who do not wish to depart so lavishly for only $250, which includes the distribution of the ashes. Yes, look ahead for a glamourous ten years of funeral pomp and ceremony – the Royal Funeral for only $1,000!

SCARCE ARSENAL!

I predict that nation after nation will cry for raw materials and will dig up those buried in metal caskets – for the metal! This shocking disregard for the dead will be only one of the many crimes to be waged against the human race in the next ten years! Russia had suggested this during the last war, but our leaders were horrified at the thought!

71

THE CONTENTED DISCONTENTS

I predict a new breed of civilians in the next ten years! The Contented Discontents!

These will be the disgruntled citizenry who are and will be content with merely complaining! They will gripe, gripe, gripe from morning until night, and yet will not do one thing themselves about it! They will gripe on the way of government, taxes, crime, sex, death costs, insurance, landlords, weather, transportation, traffic, bi-sexuality, homosexuality, heterosexuality and no sexuality at all.

You will find this breed of the discontented very happy just criticizing!

I predict that the politicians will make political hay while the discontented sunshines!

THE ISLAND OF CAST OFF WIVES AND HUSBANDS!

I predict an island will be set aside off the Oregon Coast in the Great Northwest for cast off wives and husbands who have failed their mates, and are set adrift again on the stormy sea of matrimony!

This most elegant colony will rival Reno for those on the rebound! There they will find happiness in another mate — a fellow cast off!

SWAMP FEVER IN WASHINGTON, D.C.

I regret to predict an outbreak of swamp fever in our own federal capitol, Washington, D.C.,which could easily take the toll of 250,000 lives in a very short lived epidemic! The fatal date on this will be in the spring of 1977! Beware!

OLD AND COLD

They are old and cold and condemned to death. . .for merely believing in God!

The huddling crowd of 5,000 men and women, all over 80, who worked making Canada the great nation it is today, face certain death, as they are useless, diseased, old and cold in their compound!

The Socialist state of Canada has no use for drones! In 1979, there will be much work to be done, and useless people cannot be supported, even though they have earned it!

The amazing part of this entire event to come, is that these unfortunate 5,000 have enough money to keep them, but they are guilty of taking up space in a state which needs individual action and profit if it is to continue a world power. The price we must pay for success and progress!

In the Atheist Act of 1978, each person devout in God, is classified out of aid from the Crown!

The younger tax payer, heavily burdened with back breaking amounts, taken directly* from his assigned job by the government, revolted and passed by vote the Atheist Act! This only affected those over 80, for religion had not been permitted since 1970!

They were cold and old and voted to die. . .for merely believing in God!

WHITE HOUSE GHOSTS

I predict that you will continually read reports of the White House ghosts in the next ten years — and many will prove to be authentic. Children of former presidents will be seen romping on the White House lawn in broad daylight — and actually photographed through a new camera lens! I do not ask you to believe it now...but when these events happen, please remember this prediction!

HOLLOW HEADS

I predict that the increased use of drugs in strange combinations will result in many babies being born with hollow heads. These malformations will shock and disgust every right thinking person until the point is reached where capital punishment will be given for all narcotic users, narcotic pushers and even Doctors who prescribe a certain medical area of drugs! Five years will tell!

CRISWELL ANSWERS THE 101 QUESTIONS MOST-OFTEN ASKED HIM

Q: How do you predict?

A: I predict through trend, precedent, pattern of habit, human behavior and the unalterable law of cycle. I deduct and analyze on an impersonal basis and do not permit any type of wishful thinking. You read my predictions in many of the newsletters and also my own column which is now widely syndicated.

Q: Have you chosen your epitaph and where will you be entombed?

A: I will be entombed in my home town where I was born. . .Princeton, Indiana, where the White, Patoka and Ohio Rivers converge. It will be either in the Archer Cemetery or the Odd Fellows. I am yet to decide as I have a space in both. I had chosen my epitaph "All we golden boys and girls must, as chimney sweeps.return to dust!" but now I have changed it to "World weary Criswell Predicts, Back home again in Indiana"! However I do not plan to make use of this tomb for some time, as my plans at the present time are endless!

Q: Does Medicare really care?

A: I predict that Medicare could care less, but it is your own personal demands that matter. Speak up or be let alone! I predict a Free Medicare Cafeteria, where all of the headache, toothache, stomach ache, salves or lotions, pills and cough syrups are all displayed and you take your choice free! You will be your own doctor in the future, and if you do not improve, it will be your own fault, so help yourself free!

Q: What is the biggest scandal you see in the immediate future?

A: I predict that the welfare scandal will rock the nation! Eighty-seven cents out of every welfare dollar is a fraud, and 87% of the welfare takers are taking it under false pretense. Sometimes children are collected for five times by five various people claiming to be the parents! Within three years this will be corrected and many, many will go to jail!

Q: Why do we have so much crime?

A: I predict that crime will be the number one problem as long as we prohibit prayer in the school and the mention of God on the radio and television! As long as it is considered "smart" to tear down the establishment as preached by the Red Liberals, we will have crime and more crime and more crime! Even in the depths of depression we did not have looting, arson, killing and mugging! Poverty does not cause rioting, but the evil influence of those on our youth do!

Q: What is the next important move of Red Russia?

A: I predict it will be the unifying of the Mediterranean Sea and making it a Russian Sea of influence.

Q: What do you predict about Nasser's theory?

A: I predict that money knows no patriotism and a huge Holy Roman Empire theory will be induced! I predict that the most startling headlines out of Jerusalem, Siani, the Gaza Strip, Jordan and the Suez will not deter this new Empire!

Q: What will be the whispered scandal about the wife of a famed foreign diplomat?

A: I predict that you will be told all on the front pages of your favorite newspaper and by your favorite newscaster that the wife of a famed foreign diplomat will be found guilty of operating a school for abortionists, where men and women are trained in one week for $5,000 to execute a simple abortion! Many hundreds of graduates will be picked up all over the nation carrying on this nefarious trade! Most shocking! The diplomat's wife has immunity but will be forced by public opinion to leave the country, and her husband – will be recalled!

Q: Will there be new property taxes on real estate?

A: I predict taxes will rise locally but there will be a new federal insurance to cover the cost of vacancy at a new and reasonable rate!

Q: Will privately owned mail delivery be successful?

A: Yes, I predict that many firms will deliver mail privately for the cost of five cents per letter to any place in the nation. It will go by air freight, and have delivery next day!

Q: What will be the next Japanese import to sweep the nation?

A: I predict that paper bridal outfits will be the new rage and for $1.98 the bride can look really lovely. They will come with maids-of-honor matching gowns, in seven different styles and all adjustable! Another Japanese import will be wigs for both men and women, absolutely undetectable for $5.00!

Q: Why will we not permit an Asian nation to have an airport permit in the United States?

A: This has even been discussed from the floor of the United Nations, and I predict you will soon read where this airline has been known for its stag flights, complete with off-color lascivious films in sound and color, and the airline hostesses are prostitutes. Narcotics are also available for the same price and served with the food, liquor and service.

Q: Will standards of motion picture plots change?

A: I predict the return of all-male casts to the screen, as in the old days of the westerns, for men resent seeing a brave stalwart hero submit to a woman and her domination at the end of the film! Men can always live the life of a hero but cannot accept female domination!

Q: What is the next trend in the style of protest?

A: I predict the use of children! Just as the Children's Crusade was one of the major shames of history, the use of children in the 1970-1980 periods will be just as shameful! In many of the coming protests, which face police action, the children and pregnant women are placed in the front lines so, when they are injured, it is blamed on police brutality! I predict that children will also be used to collect funds for many irregular causes, will sell spurious merchandise and also subscriptions to magazines that do not exist, to contribute to the overthrow of the establishment! Very terrifying indeed!

Q: Are Witch Doctors organized?

A: I predict they have a very strong organization in Africa, where they are a part of the ruling members of the nations. I predict there will be a move here in America where the Witch Doctors will demand recognition from the American Medical Association as discrimination will be claimed. There are many so called Witch Doctors practicing in the rural areas of many states, North, South, East and West!

Q: Do you foresee any bank crisis as in 1929?

A: The only crisis I can predict for the banks will be the flood of foreign spurious checks which will Niagara our way, and be honored, costing many innocent banks millions upon millions of dollars, making a drain on all the deposits!

Q: What real estate changes do you predict?

A: I predict that single dwellings will all but vanish from our landscape, being replaced by apartment houses, duplex and multiple dwelling courts! I also would like to offer this prediction: that many motels will become mortuaries in the next ten years, as mortuaries will be needed for the burials of the plague victims and the victims of calamities.

Q: Are we Americans in danger?

A: I predict that America is being lulled into inaction by the devious schemes of lying diplomats! The Russian-Chinese combine will bring the world to its knees in your time and in mine! Our Monitors in foreign lands continually warn of another Pearl Harbor!

Q: Many historians say we will return to the feudal plan of national-sectionism. What do you predict?

A: I predict that the shadows of coming events are already very obvious. The feudal plan simply means people living together behind locked gates and insurmountable walls for protection from others! Usually a Board of Directors or an appointed leader decides policies. Today we have communities which are walled in like little colonies, or in the cities, huge apartment houses covering blocks, in which the dwellers own their own apartments and share a community garden in the center, and the entrances are heavily guarded for protection from outsiders! Various Negro Communities have adopted this same formula. Yes, I predict we will swiftly return to the feudal plan of existance for protection and family security!

Q: Where is the millionaire's ghetto?

A: This expression has been placed on Palm Beach, Palm Springs, Cape Cod, Warm Springs but it actually originated from a very wealthy Negro settlement on the north shore of the Ohio River, the Indiana side. Negroes fleeing north before the Civil War settled and cultivated some of the most richest farm productive land in all the world there!

Q: What is the future of insurance policies?

A: I predict that within ten years the entire insurance profession will change. No longer will companies promise in large type and take it away from you in the small type! All personal liability policies will be cancelled in this period!

Q: What is the future of Spain?

A: I have often predicted that Spain would return to a monarchy, with Franco turning over the reins of the government to the Bourbons, the last of the royal line! You can expect this within three years, and it will be done smoothly.

Q: Do you predict a date for the end of the world?

A: In my previous book *"Criswell Predicts to the Year 2000,"* (Droke House, Publishers, Inc.,) I gave the date of August 18, 1999 which is also given by Nostradamus. I am a diligent student of the predictions of Nostradamus, and I may translate his prophecies soon.

Q: Why are your predictions about the British Royal Family so dire and tragic?

A: Because they are a dire and tragic family and the royal drama will catch up with them as it has other royal families.

Q: What entertainment personality do you predict will be long remembered? Which man? Which woman?

A: I predict that when the history of entertainment is written for the 20th century, one man will rise above, the present number one clown, Red Skelton. The woman? Mae West who has brought a new era in entertainment.

Q: What authors do you think will be the greatest of the 20th century?

A: Somerset Maughm, Edna Ferber and James Warner Bellah.

Q: What new trend do you predict in behavior?

A: I predict that we will enter the "Age of the Hermit" where people will seek solitude! The age of "togetherness" came to a screeching halt with the civil rights movement! Psychologists will tell you that people feel more secure when they act as individuals rather than run with the mob!

Q: What three professions would you predict for my children to follow?

A: I predict (1) sales engineering (2) electronics and automation and (3) law enforcement and crime detection! The declining professions of medicine, law and management will all be taken care of by automation and impersonal care!

Q: What do you predict about the 18 year olds voting?

A: I predict that the voting age will not be lowered but it will more than likely be raised to the age of 25! Why? The student revolution will make the nation wary of trusting them with the vote! The man and woman over 40 still controls the wealth of the nation and they will not release this power no matter what happens! You may quote this prediction!

Q: Will I ever be able to sue my Doctor and collect?

A: Yes, I predict that malpractice will be much easier to prove in the future, due to the Doctor's impersonal manner about his calling! One Doctor can be forced to testify vs. another as all diagnosis will be written out completely before any treatment is given and placed on file with the government!

Q: Will Mao be a legend of the East?

A: I predict this dissolute leader will make his name in the 20th century, and will become a legend. Virtue is not one of the virtues of greatness. Mao suffers from an incurable malady and this alone will aid him in his martyrdom!

Q: What is the future of heart transplants?

A: I predict that heart transplants will come to a very quick stop due to legal complications! The human body is not dead, actually dead, until 72 hours elapse, and by that time the organs, such as the heart, liver or kidney have become useless. It will be proven in court that many of the donors were actually murdered in cold blood by Medical Doctors for their still warm beating hearts! I predict that the Supreme Court will soon rule that no organ can be transplanted until after 72 hours to prevent murder in cold blood!

Q: What do you predict about Hawaii?

A: I predict, and regret to do so, that the Communist elements will gradually take over the government of the Islands, despite it being a 50th state of the United States! Great inroads have been made due to the mixed racial strains — and the Red Russia-Red China combine will spend millions to propagandize this take over! It will be a full ten years however, but the handwriting is in the Pacific skies for all to see and ponder. Congress will move too slow to head off the final election and the stuffing of the ballot boxes by the Red Liberals who make Communism their religion!

Q: When do you predict a dictatorship for America?

A: I predict a garrison police state for America within ten years, and it will be brought about by the anarchy of the students, the racial rioting, the looting and burning, destruction of property in a wanton manner, the hippy lawlessness, the increase in welfare recipients and other petty grafters on the government! I predict that a national emergency will be declared and all lawless individuals will be rounded up, and armies drafted for our crops which are now rotting for lack of agricultural labor. . .and law, order and justice for all established overnight! You may wonder when this will happen — and I predict within a five year period! Few will cause it, in spite of the warnings given today!

Q: When will Niagara Falls cease to be?

A: Our geologists take a dim view on the continuation of Niagara Falls, and my prediction coincides with theirs — in a scant ten years! There will be no seven wonders of the world remaining by 1988! Remember this prediction!

Q: Will California ever stop welfare families at the border of the state as they once did in the Dust Bowl incident?

A: I predict that California will stop the indigents at the border as the state is facing bankruptcy in five years! The overload of welfare takers is staggering and growing each and every day! Florida will also face the same problem, as will Arizona and New Mexico! I predict the time will come very soon when you must have permission to move from one state to another!

Q: Will there be more student rebellions?

A: I predict that the next student rebellion in our high schools, colleges and universities will be the defacing of any religious symbol or biblical quotation in, around or on any structure of the campus! Many will even find the "A.D." after a date offensive, while others will storm the statues of national heroes. Memorial windows will be broken out in a frenzy of frustration. I predict that anarchy cannot survive and it will be replaced by strict police action to quell it! I further predict that many insurance companies will cancel all coverage of public and private school buildings for any damage and will classify them as "grey-riot-areas" very soon!

Q: Will there be a race of super-men?

A: I predict there will be a planned breeding of super-men through artificial insemination now being planned by the United Nations for future generations! Here is a hush-hush prediction: I predict that through the right channels any girl or woman may purchase the sperm of a famous movie or tv star for artificial insemination by her own doctor in her home!

Q: What is the next propaganda outlet?

A: I predict that the next propaganda outlet will be over 1,000 pirate radio stations on small boats beyond the 12 mile limit both on the East Coast, the Gulf Coast and the West Coast! This will play havoc with American radio reception!

Q: What do you predict about mental defectives?

A: The increase of mental defectives due to the increased use of drugs and alcohol by the parents will result that all will be made sterile by the simple inhalation of a new and harmless chemical gas. I predict this will be a major problem.

Q: Will Russia conduct another planned starving?

A: Yes, I predict that Russia will conduct another planned starving, this time in Bombay, India and not the Ukraine Valley!

Q: Can you predict on the Peace Corp?

A: I predict that the Peace Corp will cease and their present duties taken over by Religious Missionaries from our Churches.

Q: What about Agricultural America?

A: I predict that the farmer will no longer appreciate the socialistic mismanagement of his crops and we will enter a new united "tax strike". Certain produce will be withheld, and will force the rewriting of our farm in 10 years!

Q: Will credit buying be more controlled by law?

A: I predict all credit buying will be federally controlled within three years! A new system of time payments will be introduced. Financing will be very simple. The present carrying charges and fee for late payment will be outlawed. A new low interest rate will be legally fixed. Your full credit and interest charges will be known to the penny before you sign the contract!

Q: Can you predict where the Homosexual, the Bisexual and the Hetrosexual Capitols will be located?

A: I predict that the Homosexual capitol will be Des Moines, Iowa, the Bisexual capitol will be Pasadena, California and the Hetrosexual capitol will be Erie, Pennsylvania.

Q: Will public executions ever return?

A: I predict that it is entirely possible that public executions will return as a deterrent! You will see hangings, electric chair and gas chamber executions on television under commercial sponsorship of a Memorial Park or your local Gas Company!

Q: Will the Supreme Court and the Cabinet ever be elected by public vote?

A: I predict that within ten years the members of the Supreme Court and the Cabinet will be elected by popular vote for a four year term! Democracy in action!

Q: What shocking new trend do you predict about sex?

A: I predict that the growing fad for sex is linked with the fascination of death, and more and more people will purchase caskets for the sexual act. A very famous chain store will soon stock caskets for this hush-hush purpose. The Mortuaries will object but to no avail! You will be aware of this trend. I also fearlessly predict child prostitutes of 10 and 11 years of age, either boys or girls for the depraved men and women who become jaded and desire perverse and perverted passion!

Q: What is the greatest threat to the younger generation?

A: I predict it will be mental illness! The growing local and national havoc! The loss of moral standards! The precepts of God, Home and Mother being called outdated and corny! The increasing insecurity! Radical instructors! Dubious value of study! Harmful drugs in headache and in stomach medicine! The tension and the hang-ups on every day living! Difference with elders! All lead to mental and nervous breakdowns! The restlessness, the impatience, the growing tension of despair and the forlorn attitude of negation! Mental illness cannot be taken lightly! I predict that one person under 21 out of 5 will be mentally treated within the next ten years. A shocking situation!

Q: Will there be a new drug?

A: Yes, I predict this new drug will come from ordinary clover, and will be distilled with the deathliness of the poppy! These luckless young who will be hooked on this lethal blossom will turn to crime, theft, mugging, prostitution and other sordid practices to support their habit, which could be most expensive! These children, for that is what they are, have become addicts through an adult pusher, who has made them a slave for life! One never returns from cloverism! The next stop for these depraved teenagers will be oblivion! The police will step in and stop these teenagers from destroying themselves! This of course will be called "police brutality!"

Q: What will be the next practical sport?

A: I predict it will be ocean diving theory and scuba, for this new sport can pay off handsomely! This hobby can make men well off within the year, when they apply themselves. The salvaging of sunken boats, treasures on the floor of the ocean, plus rescue and repair work can bring hundreds of dollars a day! From Malibu to Miami Beach, both men and women are learning the art of scuba, decompression, first aid procedures, ocean hazards, topography and flotation! James Evers of the Santa Monica, Calif. Scuba Technology Institute, master technician, instructs and directs some of the most perilous recovery cases on record! Scuba, the new sport! The practical sport, and a money making hobby for young and old!

Q: Will there be new rental laws for Tenants?

A: Yes, I predict that Congress will give the property owner the right to dispossess after three days for any infraction or destruction to the premises, and also for non-payment of rent! There will be no discrimination, for all tenants will be bonded in this new "open housing" plan but the renter must behave or face eviction, a fine, plus an arrest for mischief!

Q: Will everyone on welfare be listed publically soon?

A: I predict that many states will do this within the next year for the protection of others from these deadbeats! I predict that Congress will make it a federal law within a period of five years! The order will be on those who complain "get off welfare or be known as a welfare recipient"!

Q: Will we ever have a national curfew?

A: I predict that America will have a national curfew for ten p.m. each night starting January 1, 1974 after the Boston burning and the sacking of Bridgeport, Connecticut!

Q: What is the next move of the Red Liberals in Washington?

A: I predict they will seek to abolish all private schools, all parochial schools and all rabbinical colleges overnight!

Q: Will women ever be forced to take the birth control pill?

A: No, but I predict that men will! Men will gladly take the pill as it will relieve them of all responsibility and make sex safe, saving them from the designs of a designing woman!

Q: I heard you on the Johnny Carson Tonight Show predict about undersea volcanoes. Has one happened yet?

A: Yes, if you recall in late 1968, we had a series of undersea volcanoes off the California coast which caused many oil slicks and much damage to our beautiful beaches. There are many more thousands to come, and all of this heralds Doomsday August 18th, 1999, as I so carefully explained in our first book in 1968!

Q: What do you consider the most dangerous epidemic ahead?

A: I predict for Northern Africa it will be the galloping leprosy, but for America it will be chicken pox! When chicken pox strikes an adult, even blindness could result, and in some cases death! Varicella results in high fever, nodules, and a pitty face, often violent discomfort for adults, heart failure and petit strokes! Chicken pox is no laughing matter!

Q: What strange events confront us in the coming year?

A: I predict that strange radio messages from outer space will bombard us showing human super-intelligence, and establishing the fact of life on other galaxy worlds! . . .I predict that animals which have been sent to test outer space have not fared well! The super-hush-hush-secret from Russia is that when men accompanied them they saw the animals's brains burst like a fire bomb and their lungs explode with a resounding boom! This new science is still in its infancy! . . .I predict that the Russian fishing fleet off our shores will actually commandeer many private boats, yachts and vessels!

Q: What is the next move of the Treasury Department?

A: I predict that the automation will take over your tax return and give the 0-0 to all Doctors, Lawyers, Dentists, Druggists and those connected with Medicare. There will no new stern rulings! The burden will be with the Doctor, the Lawyer (free public law) the Dentist and the Druggist, not with you, the patient, or the client! You will also be asked to carry an identification card at all times!

Q: What do you predict new in music?

A: I predict a new sound — a new beat! This will take the place of Rock/Roll as this sound is dead and the market glutted with the corpses of many well meaning artists and song writers! I predict that the new beat will be known as "One World Jazz" and will inherit the musical earth! The Dixie Land Beat will live again in a more glamorous way!

Q: I am unmarried, and under my constitutional rights, I want a child. Can I force the Government to artificially inseminate me, and will they finance it?

A: I predict the Government will finance your child, but will not finance the artificial insemination. You can, go on welfare as an unmarried mother. "The Incubators", a group active in welfare, all have children but no recorded fathers.

Q: What will politicians promise next to get elected?

A: I predict they will promise a free divorce and free dancing lessons! This can be cleverly accomplished too!

Q: What will be the new rule for entering foreign nations?

A: I predict that the moment you land on foreign soil from America you will be forced to take an antiseptic bath, a shampoo and spray for lice, ticks and bedbugs. No tourist will be excused not even the personnel of the air lines!

Q: What new fortifications will be built on our soil?

A: I predict that the Canadian border will be heavily fortified. . .a new master-fortress in Mobile, Alabama for the protection from South America and Castro, plus five new arsenals on the California-Washington-Oregon coast for protection from Red China, Red Russia and the Bamboo and Iron Curtain nations!

Q: What one item will change our lives drastically in 10 years?

A: I predict it will be the new whirly-bird imported from Germany, which will be low priced, safe and economical to operate. Even a child of ten would be safe in this new and revolutionary home appliance and energy saver!

Q: If you could give one warning of personal danger, what would that be?

A: I can give you one warning – and that will concern the importing of a drug, which has not yet been fully tested on humans, but only on laboratory dogs! (which are useless and are only used for they are a source of income to a brutal debasing profession, that of pet-theft and the medical underground) This drug will be hailed as another miracle drug – but when you take it, the miracle will be that you lived! It results in a breakdown of the digestive tract, heart failure and complete insanity if taken over a two weeks period!

Q: What will be the most shocking event of the next ten years?

A: I predict it will almost sound like science fiction, but it will all be true! A South American Communist controlled nation will openly admit a hospital clinic of horrors where girls and women are bred to animals of all kinds, with very horrifying results. The sperm is built up and can be accepted by the human female womb! A nightmare of unspeakable orgy!

Q: How will the sentimental love story of our own Wallis Warfield Simpson and the Once King, and now Duke of Windsor end?

A: I predict they will be devoted even beyond death, with the Duke of Windsor demanding that he be buried beside his bride in a well known Baltimore, Maryland Cemetery, forsaking Westminister Abbey and all of the pomp and circumstance he is entitled to, due to his royal blood! This will truly make the love story of the 20th century for your children to read!

Q: Will there be another exodus to Canada?

A: I predict that over 100,000 Negroes will make the exodus to Canada to escape the coming inter-racial war within the next five years. Negroes will flee from Negro control! The "New Negro Party" which will be active in national and local politics will be most progressive and will offer a new life for millions upon millions who seek advancement!

Q: Will effigy burning ever be outlawed?

A: I predict only when they substitute the real person for his effigy!

Q: What new public service is on the horizon?

A: I predict that the broadcasting of electricity direct from the central dynamo at very low cost. Germany and Japan have had this since 1938, and we will soon have it here! No wires, poles, but just an inside arrangement the size of a pocket match box! And very, very soon!

Q: Can an Atheist teach in our public schools?

A: I predict that an Atheist will not be permitted to teach in our public schools, hold public elected office nor any civil service position! How soon? I predict Jan. 1, 1972!

Q: What new items will we enjoy ten years from now?

A: I predict we will have a purse size oxygen tank for a faint feeling or a headache. . .a pocket size two-way telephone. . .a tv set in a signet ring and a self-hypnotizer bracelet which will result in sound restful sleep with a built–in alarm clock! You will enjoy these future inventions!

Q: What is the political fate of the Liberals in England?

A: Sir Winston Churchill said once "There are no Liberals, only traitors!" and this will be proven when many Liberals (all Communists are Liberals but not all Liberals are Communists) are publically executed as traitors by firing squads!

Q: What is the next trend for Negro America?

A: I predict that the New Negro Betterment Groups will forsake "teach-ins, wade-ins, sit-ins, stay-ins" for "work-ins" where they will contract certain ventures and all donate their salaries for a common bond of establishing their own business! Racial pride will be a big factor in this new venture! Money means power and position for the Negro!

Q: What delicious scandal is in the offing?

A: I predict it will concern an English Lord who is dying of leprosy after he contaminated his wife, three daughters and many of his wife's social circle! This far reaching scandal will even shadow the jet set and cafe society!

Q: What is the new Teen-Age threat?

A: I predict it will be "spite disease" where anyone can be infected with the mere prick of a pin to implant syphilis, small pox, scarlet fever, gonorrhea, measles or malaria! This toxin is placed on the head of a pin, imbedded in a ring, and the mere brush or scratch of the skin can infect! High school students have been known to infect teachers and parents with this new "spite disease" just for personal revenge!

Q: What new rumor based on events will come out of Russia?

A: I predict that you will be very shocked at the news out of Russia and the nations behind the Iron Curtain! Under the new Socialistic Republic, any man or woman over 50 have lost their usefulness to the State and are brutally executed! The peak age is 33 and after that the person ages rapidly! When tourists visit Russia and the Iron Curtain nations this year they will notice an absence of anyone over 50! Sentiment and decency seem to have been outlawed in Russia! The Kremlin Red Masters have spoken!

Q: In the coming period of 1970-1980 what personal changes will we enjoy in our daily life?

A: I predict that the new items for 1970-80 will include (1) paper clothing at one dollar per set, for men: shirts, suits and slacks, for women: formal and informal dresses, for children: playclothing, rain-coats and togs! (2) Air coolaire mattresses which suspend you in the air for that good night's rest and relaxation! (3) A helicopter service to any airport in one minute! (4) A safe skin diving suit! (5) Oral pills for coloring the hair! (6) A full line of instant make-up for men! (7) Powdered food to which you add water! (8) Lazer light beam which removes the faulty human organs! and (9) A boom to end all booms of the Great South West with build-it-yourself housing, fashions and food for South West Living! and (10) I predict that one dollar watches will flood the nation from Japan.

Q: Is there a major change in the Kremlin soon?

A: I predict that there will be a mysterious death in the Kremlin which will be quickly denied but the ugly facts will come out in our press! You cannot suppress news, and America will remain the best informed public in the world!

Q: What is the shocking teenage craze people are whispering about?

A: I predict that the latest teenage craze is to openly steal a dead body from a mortuary, a morgue or even a hospital, dress it up and take it riding in the front seat of the car! You can expect many arrests on this new fun fad and it will be stopped almost overnight!

Q: What will be the next trend in radio and tv, business wise?

A: I predict that TV and Radio Sponsors will give definite orders to their advertising agencies NOT to buy commercial spots on any tv or radio program which campaigns for the "legalization of marijuana", is "pro-hippy and praises the student demonstrations and racial protests" and shows a disrespect for the flag, for religion and for the government! This tends to create a "subconscious boycott" of the sponsor's products as no one will buy a recommended product by a radio-tv personality supporting the new left! Yes, there will be many changes coming direct from the sponsor who must protect his product!

Q: Will national prohibition return?

A: I predict that national prohibition will be on its way back by 1974! Each state will open up their own State Liquor Laws! All liquor licenses will be renewed each year and if there is one complaint against the type of bar or cafe, the license can be withheld or withdrawn! The next step will be 100% prohibition!

Q: Are we winning the war against insects?

A: Yes, I predict we are. . .but it is a losing game in some areas, but in personal protection of the body. . .I predict that a potent new chemical, implanted in a disk and worn around the neck will ward off head lice, chiggers, flies, mosquitoes and other insects! This will be welcomed by tourists on foreign travel!

Q: Can you predict on the future of live plays and musicals?

A: I predict, at a period when the living theater is fighting for survival, some short sighted actors, stage-hands, playwrights, singers, dancers and others will decide to go out on a 100% strike. The lights of every theater will dim, and the strike will be long and futile! Fifty years ago, this strike could have meant something, but today with the night clubs, the movies, the radio and television, it will mean nothing! This will kill the professional theater as we know it today, and it will only then exist live in the colleges, the universities and the high schools! The plays will be so costly to produce with the new union costs that none will be done! I predict the living theater will out price itself out of existence!

Q: Will the new Urban Renewal Plan be successful?

A: I predict that the new urban renewal plans will meet with dismal failure! The move to the suburbs away from rioting, picketing, protesting, hippies, dope addiction, prostitution and gambling by any family who can possibly manage it will have a telling and fatal effect! The citizen who pays taxes surrenders the city to those who do not pay but collect through welfare! A crisis will arise by mid-1978 which only military law can quell!

Q: When will there be a new drive against crime?

A: I predict in the year of 1972! I predict that city by city, block by block, house by house, our nation will be covered to round up criminals who are hiding from the law and still active in narcotic selling, prostitution, petty theft rings and illicit gambling! I predict that treason and sedition through crime will be closely defined by our Congress and many, many arrests will be made soon!

Q: Is Black Nationalism on the march?

A: I predict that the Negro Betterment League will demand a division between the White/Black World with each having its own currency, banks, loan-departments, manufactured items, food, judges, policemen, newspapers, radio and television stations! This condition will be brought about sooner than you may think by the Black Power Advocates, who will receive much White aid in this undertaking! I predict that petitions will soon be on every street corner for everyone to sign! Yes, the March of Black Nationalism and Power cannot be stopped!

Q: What is beyond the horizon of the next ten years?

A: I predict that just beyond the horizon will be a new age for America! The average voter will become frustrated to the extent of "voting the rascal out" by blaming certain events on certain politicians who talk out of both sides of their mouths! I predict that both the Liberals and the Conservatives will join in dumping many office holders who play both sides of the street! Remember this prediction!. . .I predict that just beyond the horizon a new age looms for Science! In a bold advance rush, science will dominate your life in the future! Automation will solve your daily household chores, will keep books for you in your financial life, and will regulate your sexual life! Every action you take will be regulated! You will move in a world of pre-planned events! Every happening will be pre-planned! From your food diet to your physical exercise! Even pre-thought control!. . .I predict that just beyond the horizon will be a ready-made capsuled education for you! Through certain and devious medication your mind will be permitted to expand just so far and everyone will be just brimming with common sense and right thinking! You will know the right books, the right plays, the right arguments to use, and the right attitude to take!. . .I predict that just beyond the horizon will be a ready made universe just for you, based on the things you will need, not in excess but for survival!

Q: I heard you lecture in Hollywood concerning "Your Fabulous Future!" which was most thrilling. Can you give me the nine points you created at that time?

A: I predict that in your fabulous future you will (1) be able to buy a pill that will equal a seven course meal! These pills will have a slight after effect of a slight belch so you may taste the various foods which have been dehydrated! (2) that not only will the police wear his name on his badge but citizens also will be required to wear a name plate! This will protect both the police and the citizen from brutality! (3) be very pleased to know that you may dial your local operator for the continuous news service which will be on the news-wheel basis! (4) be very much in style with a close cropped hair motif, sculptured to your head and worn flat, given to the Greecian trend of classic smartness! (5) that you men and women will wear chokers of rhinestones, the men as ties, and the women as high fashioned jewelry! (6) that watermelon wine will be the new gourmet rage this winter! (7) that a new type of support hose for both men and women, costing no more than your present hose, will soon be on the market, to improve your health and cut down fatigue! (8) that a bright new hardy flower will be brought from the Andes, which will bloom the year around in any type of weather! May your winters be green! (9) and I predict that all of time payment contracts from mortages to washing machines will be uniform and you will be told the cost of your loan, with no penalty payments permitted to be charged and no extra service charges including points!

Q: On a west coast Hollywood program on tv you gave a shocking prediction about Castro. Do you recall what it was?

A: My notes show I gave the following: I predict that Castro will employ an "instant ptomaine poisoning" a powder mixed in soup which can cause death in ten seconds! This new product will be used in ridding the Cuban nation of all those over 50 who have lost their usefulness to the state! It will also be given to alcoholics, drug addicts and other troublemakers!...I predict that the entire area around Cuba has been mined with radar to prevent anyone escaping! Castro has broadened his "treason" charges to include the most minute crime, which of course results in instant death!

Q: What happened to the children of Adolph Hitler?

A: I predict that the adopted children of Adolph Hitler and Eva Braun will come back into the headlines in a coming sensational divorce out of London!

Q: Will money ever be classified as an energy unit?

A: I predict that the tides of time will bring us a new realization of the money we get for our efforts! Each dollar will be classified as an "energy unit" and those who have no expansion of energy in the past or present will find themselves legislated against! The "Have-Nots" cannot "Have" without the effort and energy!

Q: My son wants to be a female impersonator. Is there a future in this masquerade?

A: I predict that female impersonators will reap a golden harvest as fashion models, for under the new law of anti-discrimination they must be hired the same as women! I also predict that one of our new movie-tv juveniles, who will be the next heart-throb, will be found to be a girl masquerading as a boy! Do not be too shocked when you read these items on the front pages of your newspaper!

Q: Will the American farmer always be held in bondage by the Federal Government?

A: I predict that all restrictions will be lifted on the raising of food, and the farmer will find himself a free agent for the 1st time since 1933! This will be the greatest boom that the American economy will have in your lifetime! We will have hungry customers with cash in hand waiting to buy our food!

Q: Can you predict about the Boy Scouts?

A: I predict that the Boy Scouts of America will be denounced in Congress by a red liberal who will calmly claim that the Boy Scouts are nationalistic, fascistic and bent on the 100% destruction of American Rights! (Congress will hoot him down).

Q: What was the beauty secret of Marie Antoinette other than mink oil?

A: It was the fresh juice of carrots rubbed well into the skin, followed by a five minute ice pack! This old French formula will be revived by American women for beauty!

Q: What is the future of the protest march?

A: I predict that Washington, D. C. will secretly prepare for a triumphant civil rights riot! This long smoldering searing condition will come out into the open when the Leaders give the nod! They feel that this will climax the long hot summer of red rioting!. . .I predict that the next law to be passed by Congress will be that no picket, singly or in a protest parade, may carry a sign on a stick but must carry the sign without a stick! These sticks are aften weighted down with lead, which can knock out a policeman, or sharpened to a steel point which can kill when thrust! Often Molitov cocktails, so dearly loved by the protesters, can be hidden along the stick with cherry bombs, ready to be used in an instant! The Labor strike pickets have never used these lethal methods! This new ruling will be a part of the new Anti-Riot Laws now being voted upon!

Q: On the Merv Griffin TV show, you gave a most amusing prophecy of a Lord Quinley made in 1799 — can you quote it again?

A: When the world faced a new century in 1799, a group of men sat around a small table in the House of Lords in London! One man, Caspar Marsfield, Lord Quinley, made the following prediction about you and me! "In the years to come, the more the world will divide it will become closer together due to devious ways and means of quick communication which will be known instantly! (Could he have meant the telegraph, radio, tv, as instant news?) He also stated at that time that nations would ban together but would defeat their own purpose and then would disband time after time! (The League of Nations or the United Nations?) His predictions were correct but his one warning was "The most evil thing in the future is the bicycle for that will take people away from each other and break up the home!" Thank you, Lord Quinley, thank you!

Q: On a recent Mike Douglas TV Show you quoted a most interesting prophecy made on the Children's Crusade. Do you recall it?

A: When the Children's Crusade was marching through Europe and the Middle East, Ptolpar, one of the early poets of that age 1096-1099, looked into the future with a dim view. Not only did he predict the failure of five crusades but also the advent of the Dark Ages, the discovery of a new continent and the increase of death due to a plague and a series of plagues! Ptolpar also saw the roots of the Church of Rome being torn asunder and the power of the faith weakened. His predictions ended with "A powerful lawless nation will arise in East Asia (Russia) who will defy God, and bring the world to its knees in the 20th century! They will defeat their powerful purpose because they will not reward personal effort!" A very startling and shocking prediction!

LAW, ORDER AND JUSTICE!

I predict that we will turn the clock back one hundred years for law, order and justice! The Law Enforcement will break down and leave each man and woman to his own tender mercy! I predict that firemen, postmen, paper boys, teachers, store keepers, doctors, lawyers, funeral directors and police will all carry guns at all times! The days of the Old West will be revived and personal guns will be carried!

THE MIRROR DARKLY

I predict that we will look into the mirror darkly and in the next ten years we will find that (1) Religion will take on a new personal meaning, and in the strife and tribulations to come, we will identify with the Oneness of God! (2) Sex will become secondary due to the forcing of all the men and women to take the pill, which will direct our energies to other channels! And (3) Health will be the first rule of the day, for the Government will demand that we stay well, as sick and dead people do not work nor do they pay taxes!

SCANDALS!

I predict that two scandals will loom in your headlines soon! A Hollywood star will divorce his wife and marry her mother instead only to end up in a mental hospital! And I predict that a famed Minister of a fashionable church will defect to Russia with the wife of one of the richest men in all America! Her son, famous in tv, will undergo a sex change!

THE DELICATE BALANCE OF NATURE!

I predict that we will soon have a new cycle of bad weather! The protective skin surrounding our earth has been punctured, leaving us at the mercy of the elements of the thin cruel air of the universe! In our eager push for science, we have upset the delicate balance of Mother Nature, and she will turn on us in a wrathful manner! Remember this prediction!

THE NIGHT PEOPLE

I predict that a new trend in business will soon be established for the night people! Shops will remain open on a 24 hour basis, markets, beauty and barber shops, garages, and all types of services! More and more people are working at night, and this new field of customers will become most profitable! A short staff can service on a 24 hour basis!

RIOT-RAPE-REVELRY!

I predict we will soon see the end of the hollow crown now belonging to the British Royal Family! I predict that the country of England will be a scene of riot, rape and revelry! The pomp and circumstance will join the oblivion of yesterday! We shall look back in a few years and remember those were the days my friend, we thought they would never end — But they did! As one nation declines in power another rises, and that will be La Belle France, who will be restored to former Napoleonic glory and power! The French revolution of 1789 will be again repeated, only this time in England! The same things happen, but to a different cast of characters! The more things change the more they are the same! I predict that England is not through making history, and the land that begat Canute, Chaucer, Arthur, the Henry's, the two Queen Elizabeths,

Shakespeare, the Charles's, the Duke of Windsor and Churchill, will live again in Canada, and again join with America under our domination! Is there a doubter among our readers? Glance at the historical map in Ridpath's History of the World, and you can see the now wavering line growing stronger and nearer to that day of redemption! Ireland will rule Scotland and the land we now know as England, and will be a most potent world power, once it is out from under the domination of the hollow crown!

HIGH-JACKING!

I predict that high-jacking will take a new turn when the buses are high-jacked, the passengers robbed and humiliated during the long run between cities in the thinly populated areas! This new outrage will soon make headlines!

BATTLE OF THE BARTER

I predict that history will repeat itself in a new battle of the barter, where one nation trades so many matches for so many toothpicks! Bogus trading of this kind led to the pre-formation of World War II! The guilty nations will soon be known and denounced from the floor of our Congress!

RIOTING STUDENTS

I predict that rioting students, with faculty cooperation, will burn down one of our most important museums "as it is an affront to the New Left and other revolutionary groups"!

THINGS TO COME!

I predict the following events will take place in your future very, very soon! I predict that. . .A new stock market ruling will weed out many undesirable stocks and brokerage firms now on the Big Board, and create a more secure ground for investors! Note: this will not effect foreign stocks and bonds, for of these, let the buyer beware!. . .The election results will be more carefully counted and reported through a new automation process where miscount will be impossible!. . .I predict that Illinois, both the Southern portion and the Chicago area will be the scenes of riot, rape and revelry for some time to come! We cannot have anarchy and this will be established by the famous Illinois Edict soon to come!. . .The coming period of floods in the midwest! The heavy snows of the past few years, the late winters and the very late springs, add up to one total — a series of tragic floods!. . .You can expect a new series of fishing boat siezures off the South American coastal areas, which will lead to sharp action on both sides. . .Shocking decisions by the Supreme Court which will make protection of property by gunpoint almost impossible!. . .A series of quick and tragic storms in the Atlantic which will peril shipping and coastal areas as never before!

THE AUTOMATIC ATOMIC PLAGUE

I predict that during the next ten years we will be faced with what the Historians will call "the automatic atomic plague" which will sweep certain parts of the world! Our miracle men of medicine will search for a miracle to control this galloping, astounding and shocking disease!

SYMPTOMS: Slight chills due from poor circulation. Certain dizziness and loss of balance! Ravenous appetite! Cravings for pastry, rich gravies, confections and candy. Skin blotches of purple, shortage of breath and tired aching muscles will be followed by the abdominal muscles giving away and the intestines dropping to the floor, completely unattached!

TREATMENT: The patient should take to bed at once for a period of an hour, then must walk an hour to restore circulation. After the third day the intestines drop to the floor, and the abdomen is open, bleeding and could mean a certain fatality in some cases, but in others the intestines remaining grow back together, as Mother Nature mends!

DESTINATION: The destination of this epidemic-plague will cover most of the world effecting half a billion citizens of all countries. The hard hit will be the Orient and Africa, France, England and Nova Scotia.

LENGTH OF PLAGUE: I predict this automatic atomic plague-epidemic will run its course within three years and will depart as mysteriously as it came like a thief in the night who stole a half-billion lives!

NIGHT SICKNESS

I predict a new type of night sickness, the lonely aching heart which can be fatal. I predict that many thousands of lonely men and women will be found dead in bed at dawn — this new night sickness. . .the fatal lonely aching heart failure! An aggravated heart can result in heart failure!

HEADLINES OF THE 1970'S!

Famine strikes China. . .Tidal waves sweep Japanese coastal areas!. . .New outbreak in Korea!. . .British depart from Hong Kong!. . .Cambodia goes Red by combined efforts of Russia-China diplomacy!. . .Siam in new conflict!. . .East Indies periled by Communist drive!. . .Australia dissolves British control!. . .New Zealand declares independence!. . .Philippines seek statehood. . .Burma, India, Pakistan seized by Russian-Chinese invasion!. . .Russia collapses from within!. . .Israel-Arab Mid-East Federation of States shocks Europe!. . .Armenia becomes world power!. . .Spain becomes monarchy!. . .Italy become Papal State in new Anti-Communist drive!. . .Africa torn by Tribal Warfare!. . .Esperanto reestablished in international newspapers and magazines!. . .Asia in death struggle for survival against onslaught of violent weather conditions!. . .Children killed and eaten in new famine era!. . .Mysterious plagues sweep nation after nation in Asia depleting populations overnight!

FLASH!

I regret to predict the death of a world famous personality by his own hand. . .that a famed Washington hostess will soon expire from dreaded cancer. . .and that a singing and dancing blonde star will never be dismissed from a mental hospital. . .I predict that the widow of a famous British statesman will write the official biography of this great man, but it will not sell, as the interest is over!. . .I predict that cigarette advertising will be limited after the end of the fiscal year, a rumor based on an established fact!. . .I predict that the inside scandal in Washington will concern a defeated senator of the last election and his wild accusations through his growing mental illness!. . .I predict that a famed news magazine will suddenly fold much to the shock of even the insiders!

114

DANGEROUS. . .DARING. . .AND DETESTABLE!

I predict that the Church, the Chamber of Commerce and the American Legion will crack down on a dangerous, daring and detestable musical which portrays world scenes with the cast absolutely nude. The Crucifixion, Washington Crossing the Delaware, the Signing of the Declaration of Independence, Betsy Ross making the flag, the Battle of Gettysburg, the Last Supper, Custer's Last Stand, and other historical and religious events including Moses handing down the Ten Commandments — all with stark naked actors!

THE BURNING OF CHURCHES

A violent group south of the Mason-Dixon Line will organize to burn down every Church and destroy every vestige of faith and sentiment, as the prelude to a "take over" by the New Revolutionaries, within the next three years!

THE TYRANT FROM TEXAS

I predict that within five years, there will be another human tornado, a woman who will be known as the tyrant from Texas in American politics! This woman, the widow of a rancher, will be loved by all women but despised by all men for her feminine stand on all national, state and local matters! She will sweep everything in her path, and woe be the man who disputes her divine right of just being a woman!

SIN. . .SEX. . .SCANDAL!

I predict that sin, sex and scandal will rock America in five years, due to a new pagan religion which will sweep the nation! Just as LSD, marijuana and drugs take a toll of the younger population at this writing, this new pagan religion will repeat in 1975! The sacrificing of humans, a blood cult, a deviate faith and Satan's philosophy, even far worse than the present mild Black Mass, will all but wreck our sense of values in five short years! Yes, sin, sex and scandal will ride high in the sorry nineteen seventies!

THERE IS SO MUCH FUTURE GOSSIP. . .

There is so much future gossip I do not know where to begin! I predict that there will be demands that all Christmas decorations be banned from the federal capitol of Washington, D. C. and that the Christmas tree on the White House lawn be omitted. . .that every man, woman and child be tattoed with their social security number on their arm in case of national disasters. . .that all net fishing will be prohibited in lakes and rivers to preserve the fish from extinction. . .that no cash will be given for welfare, only food stamps or food itself. . .that any person on welfare committing a crime (misdemeanor or a felony) will be taken from the rolls at once during a probationary period. . .that wheat rust will spoil millions of acres of waving wheat within the next ten years, and that the new spray will prove to be ineffective. . .that the new gourmet rage will be dandelion wine, a potent healthy Indian remedy for many of your ailments. . .that a new wall paper spray over your walls will rid your house of termites, roaches, ants and even mice, and the spray is so potent it will last for five years! It is not harmful to pets nor children!

116

CONFUSION IN COURT

I predict there will be confusion in court concerning our various and sundry divorce laws which differ in every state of our union! You can be legally married in one state and just across the border of another state you are committing bigamy! I predict that within ten years we will have universal divorce laws, the same in every state! I further predict there will be no alimony, but there will be child support!

THE 20th CENTURY JOAN OF ARC

I predict the appearance of a 20th Century Joan of Arc who will lead the Negro race into the Promised Land! This valiant woman will fearlessly face the establishment and proclaim a new age! I predict a New Age for the Black World of tomorrow! The stirrings of a great destiny and realization will lift the Black World! This has already began in New York, Chicago, Detroit and Los Angeles, and will go onto make itself felt in other cities!

CLOUD OVER THE MOON

I predict that our Scientists will be concerned about a mysterious cloud appearing over the moon two years after we land there! The cloud will stay there, hiding the moon from earth view, much to the amazement of the world! Many will say it is created by living people beyond the moon to deter our new progress in space! I predict it will be Mother Nature's warning that we are going too far and to immediately stop!

AFRO-AFRO

I predict that a new potent Negro group calling themselves "Afro-Afro" (double Africans) will be the basic foundation of Black Capitalism in this country! These men are not only operating super-market-centers, factories, farms and other industries, but train all employees to be executives and managers. Crime prevention and law enforcement is also taught, and I predict that these men will be the bulwark of the Black World tomorrow!

THE BLIND SHALL SEE

I predict that within the next ten years the blind shall see with the scientific installation of tiny radar sets in the eye sockets which will relate to the brain the objects around!

TEN YEARS OF THE FUTURE

I predict that the ten years of the future from 1970-1980 will bring the following changes to you and your family: (1) A network of super-freeways, where your automobile will be fed by atomic power. (2) The use of the occult to diagnose by automation through astrology, palmistry, phrenology and physical structure to underline and prove the present medical diagnosis! (3) The use of the medicinal values in citrus, apples, pears and plums for a rebuilding of human strength after an illness! (4) The introduction of a self-healing machine which strengthens the mind and wards off the illness resulting from negation and self-pity! (5) The dating of all funds spent through a new credit card arrangement, and with a press of the button, the amount of what you owe in income tax at the end of the year will be given to you instantly! (6) That Stalin, Trotsky and Lenin will be cannonized by the Communist Party to be the Three Red Patriots or Saints, to give a Deity to this Godless creed of the 20th century! (7) That it will be entirely legal for a woman to raffle off her husband when she tires of him in the future. (8) That the end of private charities will soon take place as the Federal Government will take complete charge through a new taxation! (9) I predict the salvation of the food problem will be on the floor of the ocean! (10) A new eye disease which will cause many millions in Africa to become blind overnight! (11) A dream cabinet with lunar magnetic force will be in every bedroom of the land! The delicate vibrations will soothe your brain into a dreamful sleep and you will awake fully refreshed and will grow younger by the day and night! (12) We will have found out that we are a captive Planet, and have moved into the

119

powerful orbit of Mars which, in time to come, will mean destruction, unless we can cancel out this unnatural attraction! (13) Just as a Belle from Baltimore married the King of England, I predict that a Belle from Boston will marry another King of England in the 1970's. (14) I predict that hate, horror and hunger will soon sweep Africa. And it will not be because of war; a man-made war, but a war waged by Mother Nature, who is more cruel and brutal than man could ever be! (15) I predict that the Federal Government will summon many men and women to Court so that they may answer for many unaccounted funds of peace movements, civil rights and missionary organizations. You will be shocked at the names of the organizations where a discrepancy will be discovered! The biggest law suit in the next ten years! (16) I predict that the high water mark in floods will be reached during the next ten years when the rainfall and snow increases, with a quick and sudden thaw! And (17) I predict that 7,550 medical doctors will be arrested over the next ten years for malpractice, over-charging and illegal operations!

THE DISTANT DRUM

I predict that the distant drum will cause us to heed many things in 1970-80! I predict that among them will be the complete and revolutionary trend of the funeral profession! Grief has always been a personalized matter, and each and every mortician, funeral director and funeral advisor will undergo extensive training to psychologically conquer the feeling of loss through death! This new aid at the source of grief will do much to lift the personal burden of loss! The old time Undertaker will be replaced by a carefully trained individual which you will notice when the loss of a loved one occurs!

TV AND SMOKING

I predict that you will no longer see any newscaster or any commentator smoke on the air while conducting interviews or doing news broadcasts as the sponsors consider it a lack of respect for the viewer! It also sets a bad example for the teenagers! This new ruling will not only effect the network programming but also the local stations!

1975 FLASHES

I predict that one of our most famous tv-radio commentators will secretly have the operation at Johns-Hopkins Hospital which will turn him into a woman! This will rock the complacent world of TV!. . .I predict that, as a Civil Rights protest, many will permit their faucets to run full force for 24 hours in New York City!. . .I predict that a former Senator will defect to Russia for personal freedom!. . .I predict that 5,000 draft dodgers who are now in Canada, will be deported back to America.

THE HORNET TERROR

When future historians look back on the momentus year of
1979, one thing will be certain, and that is the full accounting
of the Hornet Family!

This vicious family of insects, fed by the gamma rays of
hydrogen manufacturing plants, increased their strength to
bullet driving power, and laid asunder many parts of the United
States!

Our miracle men of medicine and science stood by helplessly as
the tragedy unwound!

These insects were in swarms greater than the locust. The
dragon fly scare of 1976 was only an introduction to what was
to come.

Insects seemed to thrive on the mysterious power of the atomic
rays and build up a resistance to any type of poison, and were
able to resist open flame as well. The insects were taking over
the earth, while humans stood helplessly by!

The Hornet Family (*Vespidae-Polistes*) was able to build nests
in secret places, where man would never think of searching.
These evil voracious winged creatures, had the speed of
lightning, and could breed   almost as quickly. They would sting
the individual, knocking him to the ground, and inject their
deadly poison into the blood stream. After thirty seconds, they
would return in a swarm and draw the life blood, leaving the
victim a mere shell of a human body!

Many perished and then the Hornet Family vanished as
mysteriously as they came, leaving mountains of dead in their
wake.

YOUR FABULOUS FUTURE 1970-1980

I predict that in your lifetime you will see. . .personalized wings which you will wear to soar over the landscape by taking short cuts to save time. . .powdered food which you merely add water to give you the bulk you may need. . .food raised on your own walls in an organic manner overnight. . .a tiny radio which fits into your ear which you may hear news flashes or you may broadcast to anyone any place in the world. . .a tiny machine which straps onto your wrist, which keeps your body at a controlled temperature through the circulation of your blood. . .a calorie counter which rejects the calories you do not need to maintain your daily weight. . .a tiny television set strapped to your temple which throws an inner picture on the retina-pupil of your eye complete with sound. . .pills that you may take to change the color of your hair, your skin or your eyes. . .controlled driving device which prevents any accident. . .a minute mind censor which will prevent you from saying anything that you will be sorry for. . .an automated bank account which automatically rejects any check that is NSF. . .a new way to clean your clothes will be to walk through a sonic room which removes all of the dust and germs while purging your skin. . .a new method of sleep by placing you in suspended animation with a wake-up attachment to keep you on time. . .and a new happy life in the new found leisure you will have through automation!

AFRICAN BRIDES

I predict that African brides of 12 will be bought in the open market in Arabia or by mail order! These 12 year old brides will have been trained to be dutiful wives, good mothers, fine courtesans, witches, fortune tellers and witch doctors! I predict that over 5,000 will be brought into the U. S. and England in 1976.

CRIME DETECTION

I predict that crime detection as we know it today will soon advance a century overnight with the discovered use of the black light, which marks a criminal by radar, at the scene of the crime and then finds him! This remarkable new discovery can trace and find anyone almost instantly! This will first be used by the Communist Secret Police to seek out defectors even beyond the borders of Russia and the Iron Curtain nations! This can also be used for tax evasion and can ferret out dishonesty within minutes of your time!

MARIA GRACIETTE

The fabulous Maria Graciette, Chairman of the Board of Directors for International ESP in Hollywood, outlines the following events for the period of 1970 to 1980. They have been verified by the membership and accepted in their annual meetings! Maria Graciette states that cigarettes will not be permitted to advertise on the radio-tv-newspapers-magazines-outdoors and a fine of a million dollars will be levied against all law breakers. . .that the Pentagon will spend $2,000 on a machine to forecast earthquakes which will also test all ESP impressions of others. . .that the vogue of fat movie-tv stars will sweep the world, for many of the slim ones will die of cancer and of suicide because of the dangerous diet pills. . .that "Red Crystals" from Brazil to control cancer and lukemia, the solution to this long medical mystery. . .a new Doctor in California will successfully freeze dead bodies and restore them to life with a cost of $50,000. . .that the Federal Government will partially subsidize motion pictures and tv films. . .that in 1976 the Negro will establish a new Utopia in Africa with others leaving America too; Spanish, Portuguese, German, French, Italian and Hungarians, with the original Indians rising in power and importance. . .Flying Saucers will be discovered to be made by our Government with bases in Peru, Brazil and New Zealand. . .The flooding of the Arizona desert in the Tempe area, all washed away with a great loss of life. . .Marijuana and LSD legalized in 1979. . .the return of Adam and Eve like the Fathers of the Bible, wearing the fig leaf. . .the transplant of eyes, with half of the present blind people seeing once more. . .a machine that will reduce you 20 pounds in one week plus a magical cream for youthifying costing $200 per ounce. . .an escape plane to seat 800 passengers which will remove Californians when the quake arrives in 1980. The state will separate and a new isle called La Perla will rise and will bring thousands of tourists and be the new Hawaii. . .instant cooking by electronics which will outmode all stoves, gas or electric. . .a system of remote prompting for actors and public speakers, saving time and, memorizing. . .and last but not least, a new freedom of religion in prophecy plus a coming of a New Messiah out of the Desert — who will turn out to be a miserable fraud! Thank you Maria Graciette and the members of your International ESP for so clearly defining the next ten years!

THE NIGHT IS DARK

It is December 31, 1979, the night is dark and we are far from home!

We are leaving the sensational seventies and into the eventual eighties!

The prologue has become our epilogue, and Time has become a huge pot of seething lava!

Already the clouds of more wars, more deaths, and ultimate destruction are on the horizon!

America will be invaded from within, but the mighty fortress will stand!

We will emerge in 1980 without a friendly nation in the world! We will recall the words of Benjamin Franklin who told us we could not buy loyalty, respect or friendship! We will also bitterly reflect on the warning of George Washington against foreign entanglements! But it will be too late, much too late!

Let us not cry out to the Heavens, but seek the peace within, our only saving grace.

For we have but *twenty more years* of this world as we know it! TWENTY YEARS from 1979 – in the year of 1999 – all will cease.

And we will cease with it!

Criswell

1969